SELL YOUR BUSINESS

for More Than

It's Worth

More Praise for Michelle Seiler-Tucker and *Sell Your Business For More Than It's Worth*

I am very impressed with Michelle and her level of expertise. **She is truly the leader in her industry.** Her "How to Guide" is truly a remarkably fun read that **absolutely shows you how to maximize your business's potential.**
— *JT Foxx (Wealth Coach, Real Estate Entrepreneur & Radio Personality)*

This book is not just about selling your business; it's about creating a business that works for you, instead of you working for it. **Michelle is brilliant! Read her book and I think you'll agree!**
— *Mike Collier (World Renowned Success Coach)*

"Even if you are not planning on selling your business, you should read this book! **It will increase your brand awareness, grow your business, add revenue streams, and increase profits.**"
— *Phill Grove (Real Estate Entrepreneur & Investor)*

One of the key elements in selling a business is evaluating and packaging the business correctly. Pricing and packaging a business to sell for maximum value is an art form and takes an enormous amount of experience and expertise. If the business is priced too high or not packaged well, then no one will purchase it. However, if the business is priced too low, then the seller is leaving money on the table. **Michelle is brilliant at pricing and packaging businesses for sale.** She does an excellent job at fixing the existing business before she markets it in order to obtain the highest sales price possible. *Sell Your Business for More Than It's Worth* **is a masterpiece that shows you how to increase profits, plan your exit strategy, and sell your business for more than it's worth.** I highly recommend utilizing Michelle's services and reading this insightful and groundbreaking book.
— *Charles Dombek, CPA, MBA*

SELL YOUR BUSINESS
for More Than
It's Worth

GET A 20%– 40% HIGHER SELLING
PRICE FOR YOUR BUSINESS AND AFFORD THE
LIFESTYLE YOU'VE ALWAYS DREAMED OF!

MICHELLE SEILER-TUCKER

ARABELLA
PUBLISHING

NEW ORLEANS, LOUISIANA

Sell Your Business...For More Than It's Worth

Michelle Seiler-Tucker

ARABELLA PUBLISHING
New Orleans, LA

Book design by TLC Graphics, *www.TLCGraphics.com*
Cover by: Monica Thomas; Interior by: Erin Stark

Front cover photo: iStockphoto ©Flavio Vallenari
Sailboats at Mallorquîn: ©iStockphoto.com/cinoby
Maldives Boardwalk ©iStockphoto.com/cinoby
Cabo Palace ©Erin Stark

ISBN: 978-0-9859645-0-4 (HC)
ISBN: 978-0-9859645-2-8 (E)

Printed in the United States of America

This book is dedicated to my family:
My loving and supportive husband, Dr. Rick Tucker,
and my amazing daughter, Arabella Acheeana,
who is truly an answer to my prayers.

ACKNOWLEDGEMENTS

I WAS INSPIRED AND MOTIVATED TO WRITE THIS BOOK BY MY PEERS, CLIENTS AND family. I would like to thank and acknowledge all of my supporters that guided me throughout this process.

First and foremost, I want to acknowledge my clients; many of my clients have become part of my family. I have been invited into their home for the holidays, included in their weddings and the births of their children.

A big thanks to Raymond Aaron, New York Times Best Selling Author. Raymond was a tremendous asset in helping me organize all of my thoughts, ideas and experience onto paper. Raymond is a true role model, an amazing entrepreneur, a captivating speaker and inspiration to us all.

Raymond Aaron and Michelle's daughter, Arabella

I would like to thank my good friend and mentor, Mike Collier who was also instrumental in assisting me throughout my journey.

Most importantly, I would like to thank my husband, Dr. Richard Tucker for all of his love, support and encouragement. Dr. Tucker is a successful entrepreneur and truly gives back to the community.

My true inspiration and biggest motivation comes from my daughter Arabella Acheeanna Tucker. Arabella was 14 months when I wrote my book. She is now two years of age and loves to read mommy's book, which makes my heart happy.

Lastly, I would like to thank the reader; my hope is that you will find *Sell Your Business for More Than It's Worth* to be extremely informative and beneficial. I look forward to helping you navigate the delightful challenges of improving your business, planning your exit strategy and most importantly, selling your business for "MORE THAN IT'S WORTH."

Arabella reading Mommy's book

To Your Continued Success,

MICHELLE SEILER-TUCKER

TABLE OF CONTENTS

FOREWORD

I AM EXTREMELY IMPRESSED WITH MICHELLE SEILER-TUCKER'S HIGH LEVEL OF business acumen, as well as her extensive business experience. Michelle Seiler-Tucker is the leading authority in improving and selling businesses for "MORE THAN THEY ARE WORTH!" She is a true professional who is committed and dedicated to her clients' success. I am also very impressed with Michelle's passion, determination, work ethic and desire to help business owners increase their bottom line and protect their legacy.

I strongly encouraged Michelle to write a book that would share her wisdom and knowledge with as many entrepreneurs as possible. The title, "Sell Your Business for More Than It's Worth," portrays her efforts and abilities perfectly. Upon reading this powerful book, I learned she not only possesses immense business savvy, she has the unique ability to breakdown the process of selling a business into an easily understood step-by-step blueprint. Michelle walks you through her proven system by detailing the strategies to increase your profits, add congruent revenue streams, plan your exit strategy and create a business that works for you, rather than you working for it. This groundbreaking masterpiece deconstructs the mystery of how businesses are bought and sold! By reading Michelle's dynamic book, you will learn to earn more income from your years of hard work building your business, "your most prized possession!"

What makes Michelle a formidable force in her industry is that she closes nearly 98 percent of all offers she writes, and on average obtains a 20 to 40 percent higher selling price for her clients! Her remarkable track record proves her dedication and persistence; Michelle makes sure the job gets done the right way, the profitable way. While Michelle's numbers are impressive, it's her ability to create win-win situations for her buyers and sellers that guarantee her continued success. Michelle's mission is to always deliver more than is expected. She sees opportunity when many are discouraged and give up. Michelle does not give up; she identifies and corrects the top mistakes business owners make. Michelle will fine tune businesses into a "well-oiled machine" with the primary objective to sell it for the ultimate value; therefore you can afford the lifestyle you have always dreamed of and most importantly deserve!

Through our friendship, I am continually amazed and inspired by Michelle's high level of expertise and experience acquired over her career as a business broker, business consultant and business owner. She is a powerful force in the business brokerage industry, selling hundreds of businesses and franchises. In addition, Michelle has owned and operated eight very successful businesses and has now, along with her partners, franchised Capital Business Solutions.

I am delighted to promote Michelle and her book, inviting her to speak on stage during my worldwide tour of business conferences. I am confident Michelle's skills and wisdom will assist my clients in building and selling successful businesses.

I highly recommend this fascinating book as a must read! *Sell Your Business For More Than It's Worth* should be mandatory reading for anyone starting, owning or managing a business. Those starting a business will learn how to build a solid foundation from the beginning, improving your chances of long-term success and assist in planning your exit strategy. Current owners and managers will enhance their bottom-line by creating additional profit centers, managing costs and increasing productivity. In addition, this book excels with helping potential sellers navigate through the complicated endeavor of selling a business. This "how-to guide" will provide the information to build a business buyers demand! It walks you through the steps of marketing your business without breaching confidentiality, the buyer qualifying process, selecting and hiring a business broker and outlining common pitfalls to avoid. Again, I highly recommend that you read "Sell Your Business for More

Than It's Worth!" to aid in selling your business for maximum value and ensure a smooth transition.

Take a journey by reading *Sell Your Business For More Than It's Worth!* It will strategically improve your business and dramatically increase your business IQ.

RAYMOND AARON
New York Times Bestselling Author

INTRODUCTION

MANY PEOPLE HAVE ASKED ME, MICHELLE WHY ARE YOU WRITING A BOOK AND why a book on selling businesses?

The truth of the matter is that I have wanted to write a book since I was 10 years old. In fact, when most little girls were playing with their dolls, I was interviewing people and taking extensive notes in a notebook I carried everywhere. I interviewed people as if I was reporting for CNN. My mother always thought or hoped I would become the next Barbra Walters. Following in Barbra's footsteps would have certainly been a nice career. However, I have always gravitated towards wanting to own my own businesses. I am extremely pleased with the path I have chosen to walk. I feel truly fulfilled by all the individuals that have inspired me and that I have inspired and assisted along my journey.

Throughout my life, I have always been motivated to help others. I have also been extremely curious of how entrepreneurs have created businesses and made millions from their ideas and concepts.

In Chapter One, I discuss my career in sales, working at Xerox and working for Corporate America. I made a six-figure income with great benefits. However, I had a desire to build businesses and help other people obtain a better quality of life.

After many months of soul searching, I decided to start a franchise development business that I also discuss in Chapter One. I specialized in helping people purchase a franchise. During my career as a franchise developer, I was able to consult, train, support and service franchisees from all walks of life.

My background in franchise sales, franchise development and franchise consulting lead me down a strategic path of helping business owners sell their existing business. Also, I was interested in assisting buyers that were adamant about buying a business, not a franchise. I felt that I was walking away from buyers that needed my help. In addition, I encountered many business owners that wanted to sell their existing business, but did not have any idea of how or where to start. At that point, I started researching the business brokerage industry.

During my due diligence, I discovered a considerable amount of business owners that wanted to sell their businesses, however were not successful selling their own business for a multitude of reasons.

Currently, there are over 27,000,000 businesses in the United States. Approximately twenty-five percent will be up for sale at any given time. Eight out of ten businesses do not sell. Sellers either end up keeping their business, giving their business away, closing their business or filing bankruptcy.

There are millions of baby boomers planning their exit strategy and wanting to sell their nest egg so they can finally relax and enjoy their retirement or he next phase of their life. Many of these businesses will not sell, leaving baby boomers with a serious problem. This generation will be left with very little to nothing to live on if they are not successful selling their business for maximum value. This is a huge crisis facing our baby boomers and must be addressed immediately. It is my passion and mission to reach out to as many of these sellers as possible. This is one of my main objectives for writing this book.

These are startling and grim statistics for entrepreneurs that have poured their hearts and souls into their business for many decades. These baby boomers made enormous sacrifices over the years and are now faced with the most difficult challenge of all—selling their business!

In addition, sellers that attempt to sell their own business fail sixty percent of the time. Many sellers waste time, money and energy trying to sell their business on their own. Just when they think they are going to close on the sale of their business, the deal falls apart for any number of reasons. Most deals fall apart because the buyer was never financially qualified in the first place. In most cases, the seller never obtains the buyer's financials nor do they have the buyers sign the appropriate non-disclosure agreements and non-compete (if necessary). Bottom line: sellers do not properly qualify buyers, nor do they protect themselves moving forward. Most sellers provide proprietary documents and information to unqualified buyers that have not been disclosed. Therefore, the buyer is free to tell everyone they meet that the seller's business is up for sale, which can and will cause major problems for the seller and their business. In addition, prospective buyers that have not signed NDA's will also discuss the seller's proprietary information with strangers. Even worse, the prospective buyer could go out and directly compete with the seller. In my book, I offer valuable information and tips on how to sell your business and protect yourself in the interim.

As disheartening as the above statistics are, many business brokers also fail sixty percent of the time when attempting to sell businesses. It is imperative that you read Chapter Twenty, "The Top Twenty Questions to Ask When Choosing a Business Broker."

These statistics inspired me to assist sellers in selling their most prized possession: their business. I dedicated my career to assisting sellers in selling their businesses for maximum value so they can now afford the lifestyle they have always dreamed of.

In the process of selling businesses, one thing that I discovered very quickly is that many businesses will not sell for the value that the seller needs in order to build the next chapter of their life. Consequently, I work with each seller to identify the top mistakes they are making in their business in order to create a more profitable and sustainable business that will sell for maximum value. I have assisted hundreds of businesses owners improve their bottom line and create a business that works for them, rather than them working for their business.

Again, I am extremely passionate and dedicated to assisting business owners improve their business, plan their exit strategy and sell their business of more than it's worth. I love the thrill of the deal and obtaining a higher price for my sellers. Most importantly, I love to turn around businesses and assist the seller in coming up with new ideas and congruent revenue streams. There is nothing more exciting than turning around a business that was in dire need, keep families employed and continue servicing customers. Make no mistake about it—small businesses are the backbone of our economy. The more successful our small business owners are, the more successful our economy will be.

Many new and existing clients asked me to write a book about improving a business, planning an exit strategy and positioning a business in the best possible light for sell. The majority of sellers have many unanswered questions, concerns and fears that I addressed in my book. The objective of *Sell Your Business for More Than It's Worth*, is to provide much needed answers, calm the potential fears, and inform business owners that there is a proven solution to selling their business for the ultimate value.

These many requests combined with several years of industry experience, is what lead me to write this step-by-step guide. This ultimate blueprint benefits every type of business owner, manager and entrepreneur. In addition, this book is packed with many bonuses and tips that will significantly increase the reader's knowledge. Because of its immense value, *Sell Your Business for More Than It's Worth*, has received excellent reviews by leading experts and entrepreneurs.

My objective is to assist, educate and inspire readers to improve their business, plan their exit strategy and sell their business "FOR MORE THAN IT'S WORTH!"

CHAPTER ONE

What Will Make My Business Sell for Maximum Value in the Quickest Amount of Time?

I USED TO WORK FOR XEROX, MAKING A HEALTHY SIX FIGURE INCOME WITH tremendous benefits. I had the dream position in corporate America. However, I woke up one day and realized I was unhappy. I was making a ton of money for someone else. I started in sales and became one of the top sales people in a matter of months.

Typically, one of the worst things a company can do is promote their top salesman into management. I was promoted to high volume manager, managing eighty sales people. What a huge difference that was for me. Before I was in charge of me, myself, and I. I was making a good income selling and taking care of my clients. I was making a very good living doing exactly what I loved. However, I always wanted to move up and I thought I wanted to manage salespeople. But, as the old saying goes, be careful of what you wish for. I got my wish and I was thrown into a position to manage eighty unruly salespeople. My commission was dependent upon their energy, effort, and abilities. In the beginning, it was unique, fun, and challenging. However, as time went on, I found myself becoming more and more unhappy and frustrated. I

1

was not doing what I loved anymore. I was not selling, building relationships, and solving my clients' problems. I was not experiencing the thrill of the deal. I was managing a bunch of preschoolers.

One of the biggest problems with working for corporate America is having meetings to schedule meetings to actually have meetings. I was not selling anymore. I was not doing what I loved anymore. I was dealing with company politics, bureaucracy, and unruly salespeople.

Therefore, after months and months of frustration, I decided to do something about it. I could have gone back into sales for Xerox and relinquished my management position. I'm not the type of individual that can go backwards. My motto has always been "No rearview mirror." I don't look back! I don't like to look at should of, could of, and would of. I don't go backwards.

Thus, out of my unhappiness, frustration, and need for change and growth, I decided that I would buy a business and be my own boss. But it could not be just any business; it had to be a business that heavily involved sales and solving problems. I looked at several businesses; however, none of them had the sales component that I was looking for. I stumbled across a company that was in its infancy stage of franchising their business. They had the cookie cutter formula, the training, support, and brick and mortar franchise. They were having a very difficult time getting their feet off the ground. I was interested in purchasing their franchise. They had a few company-owned stores and they gave away a few franchises for practically nothing. They were having tremendous difficulty selling their franchises. After numerous meetings and conducting my own due diligence over a period of months, I decided I could help them develop and sell their franchises.

Therefore, I did not purchase their franchise, but I negotiated an agreement to join forces. I started my own franchise development company and sold their franchises. I left my position with Xerox and never looked back.

My colleagues, friends, and family thought I was insane! They thought I had lost all my marbles. Who does that? Who gives up a six figure position with phenomenal benefits to start a franchise development company and sell franchises for and with a company that has not been successful at selling their own franchises? My friends, family, and colleagues would tell you that no one does that! That is a huge mistake; it's similar to jumping off of a 150 foot cliff without a helmet and parachute. However, I did not listen to all their negativity and their unsolicited advice.

> One thing that I had going for me—that so many other Americans don't—is that I knew my strengths and weaknesses.

I can now tell you that it was by far the best decision that I have ever made! I could have done what hundreds of thousands of Americans do, which is stay in their miserable jobs and complain to other miserable people. Misery loves company.

One thing that I had going for me—that so many other Americans don't—is that I knew my strengths and weaknesses. I knew what I was good at and I knew what I loved to do. I love the thrill of the deal. I love to build relationships that last a lifetime, and I love to solve my clients' problems.

Within six months I was generating more income than an entire year with Xerox. I knew I had made a great decision and I was doing what I loved. I sold several hundred franchises. But then something happened; after selling franchises for a few years I realized that my philosophies were very different from the franchisor that I was representing. My philosophy is to under-promise and over-deliver. Their philosophy was quite the opposite of mine. I found myself in a terrible quandary. I was selling this tremendous package of service, training, and support, and the franchisor was falling dramatically short in servicing their franchisees. So I was doing what I love: selling and building lifetime relationships with my clients. However, I was not solving problems because the franchisor was causing more problems by not meeting my clients' needs and not fulfilling their commitments.

That is when I decided that I could not represent that franchisor any longer. I could not look myself in the mirror and sell their products and services in good faith because they were neither servicing my clients nor were they listening to constructive feedback and take care of the franchisees' needs. Needless to say, that franchisor had huge issues to deal with. That is when I started my business brokerage firm, which specializes in selling businesses new and existing franchises. Since opening my business brokerage firm, I have sold several hundred businesses, existing franchises and new franchises. I am doing exactly what I love to do, which is helping my sellers plan their exit strategy and helping buyers purchase their legacy. I'm helping buyers buy the American Dream. I'm helping buyers to have financial freedom, be their own boss, and have a better quality of life.

> I'm helping buyers to have financial freedom, be their own boss, and have a better quality of life.

I have owned eight different businesses. Since opening my business brokerage firm years ago, I have joined forces with three other dynamic business brokers and licensed our company. We currently have several business brokerage offices throughout the United States and are growing. We are teaching other individuals interested in becoming business brokers how to sell businesses the correct way. Unfortunately, like any other industry, there are good and bad business brokers. My firm provides a business brokerage training program that is unparalleled in the industry. We teach up-and-coming business brokers everything from A to Z when selling businesses and assisting buyers in buying businesses. My firm's goal was to train and mentor business brokers in order to create a much more professional group of business brokers to better service sellers and buyers. I preach and teach constantly that when you sell someone's business, you are selling their life's work, the sacrifices they have made, the time, energy, effort, and money they have poured into their business for years and in some cases even decades. You are not just selling their business; you are selling their legacy, their nest egg, which will now become their retirement fund. I tell business brokers "Selling someone's business is not something you should enter into lightly without proper training, good business acumen, and a mentor to assist them along the way." We will discuss this further in Chapter 20: how to interview business brokers, detailed questions you should ask, and things you should look for. It is imperative to hire an experienced business broker, not an order taker. I will discuss the difference between order takers and professional, experienced, business brokers throughout the book.

Due to years of experience, I have worked with all levels of businesses. I have sold businesses that are barely hanging on. You have heard the old saying "someone else's junk is another man's treasure." I have sold businesses that are making huge profits, and I have sold businesses that have been around for decades. I have helped sellers through divorces, relocations, burnout, bankruptcies, and I have helped sellers on their death bed. I also have worked with all types of buyers from all walks of life. I know what will sell, what won't sell, and most important, I know how to maximize my seller's value.

Most buyers look at a multitude of characteristics of the business that they are interested in. We will discuss these characteristics throughout the book.

Some buyers will purchase the business if the business does not meet certain criteria and other buyers will not.

There are five different types of buyers:

First Time Buyers

There are millions unemployed who have to replace their income. Many of these buyers have been laid off from their jobs and corporate America.

They need to replace their income; they do not have a choice. Many of these buyers are utilizing their retirement funds to acquire a down payment to purchase a business. There are resources available to assist buyers in purchasing the business of their dreams by utilizing their retirement funds without paying taxes and penalties. The majority of these buyers will enlist the services of a professional business broker to help them navigate through the buying process. Many of these buyers are green and are not familiar with the intricate details of buying a business. Many of theses buyers will not pull the trigger unless they feel safe, protected, and feel confident that they are making a good decision. A business broker can assist in eliminating fear, protecting their interest, and providing peace of mind.

Sophisticated Buyers

Most of these buyers are experienced in buying, starting, and running businesses. They know the pitfalls of buying and starting businesses. They understand business evaluations. They understand how to cut to the chase and determine if a business is making money or if the seller is trying to pull the wool over their eyes. These buyers also understand that most good businesses are listed with a business brokerage firm and they will work with business brokers to show them good businesses that are properly evaluated to meet their buying criteria. These buyers know what they want and pull the trigger fairly quickly.

Strategic Buyers

These buyers typically buy businesses that are in the same industry. Or they purchase businesses that are a good strategic fit to their current business. A lot of strategic buyers will buy similar businesses to add additional profit centers, create additional revenue streams, or solve a particular problem they are having in their current business. They will also buy businesses to be able to fulfill the demands of their existing client base. These buyers are sophisticated and know exactly what they are looking for. They too will solicit the assistance of a business broker to help them locate businesses that meet their needs and buying criteria.

Turnaround Specialist

These buyers seek out businesses that are doing poorly so they can fix them, generate a profit on them, and in most cases turn around and sell them. They find distressed businesses in a multitude of ways. But, they too will hire a business broker to bring them distressed sellers.

Private Equity Buyers

These are great buyers because many of them have disposable income and funding in place. They constantly send business brokerage firms a list of businesses they are interested in purchasing. Professional business brokerage firms will sort these equity firms by industry, location, price range, and net income range. This is the most effective way to match sellers with private equity buyers. My firm currently works with over twenty five hundred private equity firms.

Which buyer will be best suited to purchase your business?

That will depend on the following points that I will discuss in great detail. When you decide to market your business for sale, there will be several items for you to consider. To maximize value and determine what group of buyers is right for your business, you may choose to engage the assistance of a professional business broker. Experienced business brokers will have a database of buyers sorted by the five types of buyers we mentioned earlier. All business brokerage firms should have a database that sorts all buyers based on industry, location, price range, down payment requirement, net income requirement, and time frame.

As mentioned earlier there are five types of buyers. In determining what type of buyer is right for purchasing your particular business we will need to examine the following areas in great detail. Listed below are common questions that all buyers ask brokers and sellers. It is important to have the answers to the buyer's questions before putting your business on the market. We will explore each specific area in the next several chapters that buyers examine and questions buyers ask before they choose to look at your particular business.

- **Industry:** What is your industry and are buyers attracted to it? Are you in a competitive industry or a niche market? Is your particular industry fading or on the cutting edge?

- **Years in Business:** How long has the business been in existence and how long have you owned it?

- **Do you have partners, a board of directors, or stock holders?** Is everyone on board with selling?

- **Client Base:** What does your client base consist of from a demographic and geographical base? What is your customer retention rate? Do you have contracts in place?

- **What is your product mix? Is your business seasonal?** Do you have any trade secrets and or trademarks?

- **Location, Location, Location:** Truth or myth to running and selling a business? Is your business home-based? Do you lease or own your space? Can your business be relocated?

- **Do you own the real estate?** Will you sell your business with or without the real estate? Do you have a recent appraisal?

- **Employees and good management:** These are the biggest and most expensive problem in any business. How many employees do you have? Are you a sole proprietor? Can your business run without you?

- **Financial records:** Do you have clean financials? Do you show a profit? Do you know what you make and what you run through your business? Do you take a salary? Are you up to date on your taxes? Are you reporting everything?

- **Do you operate on a calendar year or fiscal?**
- **How does your business look?** Is it cluttered, does it need painting or new flooring, does it need a facelift?
- **Do you have a lot of FF&E (furniture, fixtures, and equipment)?** How old? Is it all in good working condition? Do you owe any money on your FF&E? Do you have an appraisal on FF&E?
- **Is your business predicated on inventory?** Are your shelves or racks stocked or does everything look empty?
- **Do you have Accounts Receivable?** What are your average receivables? What is your average collection rate?
- **What is your Accounts Payable?** What is your debt?
- **Why are you selling?**
  - Retirement
  - Health Issues
  - Burned Out
  - Relocating
  - Divorce
  - Business decling, losing money

Your answers to all these questions and more will really dictate what you can sell your business for. Buyers will absolutely want to evaluate all of these characteristics of your business in order to determine if your business meets their buying criteria and if your business is worthy of the price tag you are listing if for.

It is imperative to strategically think and plan for all the intricate details that buyers will examine and review when evaluating your business. The more prepared you are to address buyers' objections up front, then the better equipped you will be to handle these objections and obstacles when they occur.

CHAPTER TWO

Is Your Industry Desirable to Buyers?

Is your industry on the way up or the way out?

THIS IS A VERY IMPORTANT QUESTION FOR ALL SELLERS TO PONDER. THERE ARE A lot of industries that are practically a dying breed. According to *The Wall Street Journal*, the following 10 industries are unlikely to ever fully bounce back from the recession: Wired Telecommunications Carriers; Mills; Newspaper Publishing; Apparel Manufacturing; DVD, Game and Video Rentals; Manufactured Home Dealers; Video Postproduction Services; Record Stores; Photofinishing; and Formal Wear and Costume Rental. There are many industries that are thriving and are on the cutting edge, such as VoIP Providers, Wind Power, E-commerce and Online Auctions, Environmental Consulting, Biotechnology, Video Games, Solar Power, Third-Party Administrators and Insurance Claims Adjusters, Correctional Facilities, and Internet Publishing and Broadcasting. And there are those industries that have been stable for decades and will continue to thrive and not take a nosedive.

Can your business/industry be duplicated or franchised?

Is your business/industry something extremely unique with very little competition? Throughout my career, I have worked with a multitude of sellers who wanted to sell their business because the challenge was gone. They have done everything that they felt they could possibly do to grow their business to the next level. They wanted to sell so they could take the revenues and go create their next masterpiece.

When I sit down with my sellers, I look at all their reasons for selling, the problems they are experiencing, their options we can explore to create their exit strategy and solve their immediate problems. Many times I was able to evaluate a seller's business and seller's concerns, need for change and complete boredom. I was able to sell my client's business and assist them with franchise development. If a seller is bored and lacks challenge, but they still like what they do and they still believe in their products and services, then I can help them sell their existing business. They can then utilize the profits from the sale; I can then help them create a franchise and grow their company using other people's money. This opens up a whole new world of possibilities. Not only is the seller continuing their legacy and helping their clients, they are also providing an opportunity for other individuals to own a piece of the American Dream and flourish in the business they first created.

Do you have any trade secrets?

The more trade secrets/trade recipes, the more proprietary systems that you have in place, then the more desirable and valuable your business will appear to buyers.

Do you have any trademarks?

Trademarks, trade logos, trade slogans, and trade products are very valuable to buyers. These trademarks make a company much easier to franchise and duplicate. YOU can obtain a much higher multiple of profits for your business if you have trademarks and proprietary systems in place.

How many revenue streams do you have?

When a company has multiple sources of income and multiple profit centers, that company becomes much more attractive to buyers. Many businesses go out of business every year because all their eggs are in one basket.

What special skill sets and licenses are needed in your particular business/industry?

Every industry is different and requires a different set of skills. Most first time buyers tend to purchase a business that they believe is easy to own and operate. Make no mistake about it; there is no such thing as any business that is easy to own and operate. Owning and operating your own business is hard work. That is why so many businesses fail in the first five years of being in business (over 50% according to the Small Business Administration). First time buyers gravitate towards coffee shops, cafes, restaurants, bars, Laundromats, convenience stores, and day cares. These are not easy businesses to operate; however, they are easier than many businesses that require special skill sets and specialized training. Technical businesses requiring specialized skill sets and licenses are more difficult to sell. They are more difficult to find qualified buyers and more difficult to obtain lending because all lenders want buyers to have industry experience. It is very difficult for a buyer to buy an air-conditioning and heating company if they are not experienced and licensed in air-conditioning and heating. The company may have employees in place, but what happens if the employees walk out of the business? Then the owner will be in a pickle. Some industries require special licenses that the buyer will have to obtain before he or she closes on the business.

How long will it take you to train someone in your industry/ business?

I have seen businesses of every size and level that are interested in selling. This is a very important question for a business owner to ponder. A convenience store might only take a few days to train someone. If the buyer has convenience stores, then the seller might not have to train the buyer at all. Obviously, the level and time frame of training will depend greatly on the industry and the skills and experience of the buyer. Some industries and businesses will take weeks, months, and even years to properly train the buyer and ensure a smooth transition. Therefore, you need to ask yourself, how important is my role in the business? Am I the business? Do the company relationships depend on me? What happens when I am not involved in the business? Can the business sustain itself and run without me? I will go into greater detail as it relates to employees and management team in Chapter 6. How difficult is it to learn my particular industry? What type of buyer do I envision buying my business? How long am I willing to stay on to train the new owner? Most small businesses only require 1-4 weeks of training. Medium size businesses usually require 2-4 months. Training is always included in the sale of the business. Larger businesses may require the owner to stay on with pay for 1-5 years, again depending upon the size of the business and the relationship with the owner, and his/her clients. Every deal is different and has to be evaluated on a buyer by buyer scenario. Years ago I sold a multimillion dollar dental lab. This company had been in business for twenty plus years. The owner specialized in producing

crowns and veneers. The seller had seven techni-
cians and administrative staff. The owner had a
business, not a job to sell. He had built strong relationships with dentists over the past twenty plus
years. These doctors looked at him as if he were the
"business." They continued to send business to the
owner based upon their relationship. The owner's
last name was actually the company's name, which
could cause problems as well. I was conducting my
search for the proverbial needle/buyer in a haystack
that met all the seller's qualifications. I was able to
find a qualified buyer that was motivated and had

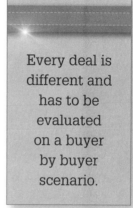

Every deal is
different and
has to be
evaluated
on a buyer
by buyer
scenario.

money. Yippee, that is the hardest part! The buyer did not have any experience in producing crowns and veneers. However, the buyer had
years of sales experience in the dental community. The buyer was very
interested in moving forward, but would only do so if the seller agreed
to stay on for five years. The buyer felt that it would be detrimental to
the business if the seller did not stick around for a period of time. The
seller had absolutely no intention of staying for five years. In fact, he
was adamant that he would only stay on for a year. Therefore, I had my
work cut out for me. I had to structure a deal that would work for both
the buyer and seller. The buyer would not buy unless the seller agreed
to stay. The seller was not willing to stay for five years. I had to find out
what it would take to keep the seller on for more than a year and structure a creative proposal around everyone's wants and needs. I structured
an offer that included so much cash upfront, seller financing, a five year
earn out; based on productivity and efficiency. I also negotiated a five
year salary for the owner at $100,000 annually. The seller had to work
full-time for the first years and part-time for subsequent years. At the
end of the day, the buyer's concerns were addressed by having the seller
agree to stay for five years, and in order to receive additional profits the
seller had to assist the buyer with increasing revenue and controlling

cost. The seller was ecstatic, because he earned a lot more income by agreeing to stay for five years on a part-time basis, and he was able to transfer his baby over to a good quality parent. Therefore, his customers and employees were taken care of. Everyone wins: the seller, the buyer, the clients, and employees.

The top five industries that are in demand:

- Elder Care
- Health and Wellness
- Warehousing
- Shipping/Logistics
- Outsourcing/Staffing

To see **WHAT INDUSTRIES ARE SELLING,** visit
www.betterbusinessbrokers.com
(877) 853-4227

CHAPTER THREE

The More Years in Business, the Greater the Return

THERE ARE 27.5 MILLION BUSINESSES IN THE USA AND 99.7 PERCENT ARE SMALL businesses according to the Office of Advocacy estimates. Small Businesses employ about half of the U.S. workforce.

Fifty percent of businesses fail in the first year. This number is claimed to rise as high as 56 percent in the first five years. There were 641,759 businesses that opened in 2010 and 813,353 closed in 2010. There were 56,282 bankruptcies in 2010, as well.

More than half of new businesses failing within the first five years is a significant number! Primarily, businesses have a difficult time making a profit in their first five years of business. Almost all businesses experience a loss when first beginning, and it is often several years before they can show a profit. New investors may not be willing to deal with these losses, and the business may not have enough capital to weather the financial storm.

Secondary reasons that businesses fail are far more strategic. Businesses are sometimes begun for the wrong reasons, whether solely as a means to make money or for continuous success, and owners may not have the passion or persistence to keep running the business efficiently and learn from their mistakes.

Dreamers set themselves up for failure, not success.

Many other factors can affect business success in these first years, including management philosophies and bad locations. Many individuals start businesses, such as dress shops, gift shops, coffee shops, cafes, restaurants, day cares, and more. They believe that their particular business will be successful because it is their passion. They believe that if you do what you love then the money will follow. That belief system might be true for a limited few, but unfortunately it is not true for the majority of business owners. I don't call these individuals entrepreneurs; I call them dreamers. These dreamers believe their ideal and concept to be good and desirable to patrons. Dreamers believe that their ideal and concept is unique; most of the time, it is not. They basically believe in the "build it and they will come" theory. These dreamers do not do their research or conduct any due diligence whatsoever. Dreamers do not have experience running or starting a business. They do not pull demographics, they do not have a business or marketing plan, and they are all severely undercapitalized. Dreamers set themselves up for failure, not success.

Again, there are over twenty seven million businesses in the USA. At any given time, twenty five percent of them will be up for sale. Eighteen to twenty percent will actually change hands annually. That is over four million businesses changing hands every year.

Unfortunately, a lot of the businesses that are up for sale are failing because of the dreamer's mentality and poor business operations. Please don't take this the wrong way when I refer to dreamers. I am a huge believer in entrepreneurship, and I absolutely respect entrepreneurs.

Entrepreneurship is alive and well and accounts for employing the majority of half our workforce. I live, eat, and breathe entrepreneurship. However, I do not believe individuals without any business experience or proper working capital should start a business! It is a huge crapshoot: the majority will fail, and only a few will succeed. For the majority who are not successful, it is a drain on their pocketbook, a drain on our society, and it cannibalizes the marketplace, making it more difficult for experienced business owners to make profits. I believe dreamers should buy an existing business with years of experience, proven track record and a healthy client base and cash flow.

There are millions of Baby Boomers that have been in biz for 30 to 45 years. These Baby Boomers have solid businesses that have been around for decades. These Baby Boomers have weathered all kinds of storms, both internal and external. They have been through Mother Nature's storms, financial storms, competitive and political storms. These Baby Boomers have grown and nurtured their businesses over the past 20-60 years. These Baby Boomers have made tremendous sacrifices over the years. They have poured their money, time, energy, and effort into their business. They have sacrificed time with their family, holidays, and vacations. Many of these businesses still have a great concept, loyal customer base, excellent name recognition, and brand awareness.

When selling a business, your business is going to fall into one of four categories. It is imperative to determine which category your business falls into.

The Dreamer Category

Again, unfortunately these are the majority of businesses up for sale. These businesses are not doing well and don't evaluate enough for the dreamer to recoup their investment. However, don't give up on selling this type of business. My office takes these listings all day long. The current owner might be out of working capital, time, and patience. But the business still has a client base, FF&E, and inventory. As I had referred to in the previous chapter, there are buyers for businesses that are not doing well. There are turnaround specialists that love to buy fixer-uppers. In addition, there are always buyers that think they can do a better job than the current owner. Usually, they are wrong, but who are we to say they cannot do a better job? If they can afford to buy the business, have money left over for working capital, and think they can do a better job, then by all means let them give it the old college try. Keep in mind: These businesses are not going to sell for top dollar. You are not going to be able to maximize value and get the highest multiple possible. A lot of these businesses are losing money and will most likely sell for the value of their assets and inventory and perhaps a little cash flow.

The Businesses That Have Been Around for Five to Twenty Years

These businesses are doing much better than the previous category. These businesses have weathered the five-year financial storm. Most of them are doing well and are making a profit. Sellers sell these types of businesses for a variety of reasons. A lot of sellers get what I call "the seven years itch." They sell because they are truly entrepreneurs and they become bored with their business. They are still young enough and still have plenty of energy, motivation, spirit, and fight in them to go out and create their next masterpiece. Depending upon all the intricate details, these businesses will in all likelihood sell for a good profit. We can usually maximize value when selling these types of businesses.

The Businesses That Have Been Around for Decades with Mutiple Owners

However, these businesses have had multiple owners. These too are great businesses to sell. They have a proven track record, a loyal client base, and are typically making good profits. These businesses are worth a higher multiple and will absolutely sell for a profit as long as the business still cash flows.

The Businesses That Have Been Around for Decades with the Same Owners

These businesses have been around for decades with the same owner or the business has stayed in the family. These are typically the best businesses to sell. Of course with any business, there are strengths and weaknesses. The glaring weakness of these businesses is the fact that the owner has been around for so long. The age of the owner and skill sets will determine if the business has become antiquated or kept up with the changing times. If the owner has hired new blood with a different set of skills that can bring the business into this century, then the business will maintain its value. If the business is antiquated, then the new owner will certainly take into consideration the cost of bringing the business up to speed. As long as the owner has kept up with the changing times and technology, and has reestablished itself to not only appeal to its current clientele but new clients as well, then this business will sell for maximum value. Out of the four categories of businesses for sale, this could be the most valuable. It really depends on how the business is doing with the original owner after all these years.

Again, all factors have to be taken into consideration when selling your business. I listed a welding supply business. The seller had owned the business for decades, and was still doing well and generating a profit. However, the business was very antiquated. Every single client was in a Rolodex. They had hundreds of customers organized in several different Rolodexes. They have extensive inventory that was written on pieces of paper. They had no computers and everything was done the old-fashioned way. Heaven forbid if there was ever a fire! The new owner needed to calculate how much it would cost them in time, money, energy, and effort to input all this data into a contact management system and bring the company up to the 21st century. This business was certainly salable. It just needed a facelift. I consulted the seller on what they needed to do before we listed the business. The seller was up in years and did not want to make the investment and spend the time necessary to computerize his business. Therefore, he decided to reduce the price of his business to compensate the new owner for making the changes. That is the bottom line; you can consult with my company or another consultant to implement changes, policies, and procedures or you can simply take less for the business. In the end, it is your choice. Most sellers will choose to fix and turn around their business in order to maximize value.

To sum up this chapter, the longer you have been in business and weathered all the storms and if your business still does well and makes a good profit, then you will be able to maximize value and sell for the highest multiple.

However, if you have not been in business for years, don't get discouraged. There are ways that you can increase revenue, gain market share, and embrace other factors that are important to buyers and are imperative to maximizing value. There are consultants, such as myself, that work with sellers before they put their business on the market to assist them with implementing all the factors that buyers will evaluate when buying businesses.

In order to **IMPROVE YOUR BUSINESS BEFORE YOU SELL YOUR BUSINESS,** visit
www.betterbusinessbrokers.com
(877) 853-4227
for a **FREE CONSULTATION.**

CHAPTER FOUR

Customers are the Fuel in Your Business; Without Them You Run Out of Gas

THUS FAR IN PREVIOUS CHAPTERS, I ASKED A LOT OF QUESTIONS. KEEP IN MIND the questioning is not going to stop. The buyers will ask a multitude of questions before, after, and during the selling process. You have to ask yourself all the questions in this book and then some if you want to sell your business and desire to obtain maximum value. Professional, experienced business brokers constantly ask and probe the business owner in order to assist the seller in maximizing value when selling and/or to assist the seller in fixing the businesses so that it can be sold for the highest possible price.

- Who is your client base? Do you have residential or commercial clients? Do you have wholesale or retail clients? Without an inventory of clients/customers, you do not have a business to sell, nor will you be able to stay in business.

- What is your company's relationship with your clients? Do you have a one- on-one relationship with your

customers or do you barely see them? Are your clients loyal to you, your products, and services?

- What are the demographics of your clients? What is the age of your clients? Are the majority of your customers older? If so, you might want to explore some options to market your products and services to younger generations. Is your customer base mostly younger individuals who do not have as much disposable income?

  If so, you might want to market your products and services to Generation X and Baby Boomers who may have more disposable income. It is prudent to market your products and services to a wide range of generations; therefore, you are not putting all your eggs in one basket. If your basket of customers breaks, then you are out of business. Are the majority of your clients female or male? Are your products and services gender specific? Or are your products and services versatile enough to appeal to the masses?

- Who can afford to purchase your products and services? Do your products and services appeal to blue collar individuals or individuals with a higher disposable income?

- What is the geographical area in which consumers travel to buy products or services from your business? What is the radius in which your products and services pull from? Can you expand your marketing to attract buyers from a larger radius? Or can you invest more advertising dollars into local/niche market areas to increase visibility and gain more market share? Does the increase of gas prices cause your clients not to travel to your business to purchase your products and services? If so, can you sell to your customers via the internet and ship products directly to them?

- What percentage of your business is repeat business? Do you have loyal clients that have been buying from you for years and years and years? Do you have customer contracts in place?

Typically, 80 percent of business comes from 20 percent of our clients. Is this rule of thumb applicable in your business? Do you have a huge percentage of your business tied up in one or two customers? If so this could be a huge issue in your business and will send up "a red flag" to buyers! This is not good for business. If you lose that one customer, you could be out of business! Buyers will explore your client mix in the due diligence phase. Buyers look for a diversified customer mix. They don't want the seller's products and services to be tied in to one or a few customers. Buyers know if that client leaves, then the business will take a huge hit and, in all likelihood, go out of business.

Having to replace customers is one of the most expensive line items in business.

I listed an office supply company that had been in business since the fifties. Sixty percent of their business was tied up in government contracts. These government contracts are negotiated by a third-party company and typically renewed every two to three years. However, twelve percent of their business was coming from a seller's negotiated contract. This contract was ending in a few months and another contract that represented five percent of the seller's business was ending in a few days. The buyer negotiated an offer that would provide a price reduction if the seller could not renew these two contracts. The adjustments would decrease the amount of seller financing payments due to the seller monthly. Buyers are looking for the seller to give concessions if there is a chance that the revenue could decline based upon customer base.

How many clients do you lose a year? How much money does it cost you to obtain a new client? Typically, having to replace customers is one of the most expensive line items in business. Do you lose customers due to the economy? Do you lose customers due to poor service and lack of quality control. Do you lose customers due to employee turnover? What is your retention rate? Are your clients loyal and continue to buy from you? Do your clients speak highly of you and refer your products and services to their friends, family, and colleagues? What percentage of your business comes from referrals? What is your occupancy rate?

If you are selling a hotel, B&B, day care, or education business, most buyers what to know what your occupancy or capacity rate is. If your occupancy rate is high, then you will obtain a higher selling price. If your occupancy rate is low, then you need to figure out the problem and stop the bleeding. Otherwise, you are going to have to sell at a loss. Again, there are turnaround specialists such as myself that can help you improve your business before you sell your business.

To learn **HOW TO INCREASE MARKET SHARE**, visit
www.betterbusinessbrokers.com
(877) 853-4227

CHAPTER FIVE

Is Your Business Based on Brand Loyalty or Location Loyalty?

EVERY BUSINESS IS UNIQUE. SOME ARE PREDICATED ON LOCATIONS AND OTHERS are not. It really depends on the industry. Most retail businesses are absolutely dependent on location, and moving the business could be detrimental. People – especially customers – don't like change. Consumers come with a set of behaviors, habits, and routines that are sometimes impossible to break or change. It really depends on the brand loyalty that the particular business has with their clients/customers. If the business truly has brand loyalty, then the clients will follow. If the business does not have brand loyalty, then they won't. It's that simple. I have seen businesses relocate and that business does not miss a beat. They keep on making money. I have seen other businesses relocate and go out of business. You need to know your business. Does your business have brand loyalty or is it predicated on your location? Below are more questions, thoughts, and ideas you should ponder before pricing your business and putting it on the market.

Do you have a brick and mortar location?

If so, how long has your business been located there? Is your business in a high traffic area? Does your business have a lot of visibility? Do you have lots of signage? Are you in a strip mall with high visibility anchors, such as Target, Walmart, or Office Depot? Do prospects constantly walk by your business on the way to a coffee shop or grocery store?

Is your business predicated on location?

As mentioned above, this is a good question to ask yourself. Do you have brand loyalty or location loyalty? If you answer location loyalty, then I hope you have a long-term lease with lots of options and great terms. I also hope your lease is transferable and/or you can sublease. If your business is dependent on location loyalty and the buyer cannot transfer the lease or negotiate a new lease with the landlord, then you have nothing to sell! It is obviously better to have brand loyalty versus location loyalty. Brand loyalty is powerful. You never know what may happen to your location. Locations are vulnerable to storms, fire and crazy landlords. If your business is predicated on location, then make sure your lease is recorded. I have witnessed horrible situations where the business owner's lease was not recorded and the landlord sold the building, and the new owner of the building evicted all the tenants. I will not take a listing if the business is predicated on the location and the lease is not transferable or the landlord will not allow a sublease or negotiate a new lease. It is almost impossible to sell a business if the business owner is on a month-to-month and the landlord will not negotiate a new lease. Landlords can make or break a deal. Keep in mind that if you put your business on the market and have a month-to-month lease, then the buyer can and will go behind your back and negotiate with the landlord, and there is nothing you can do about it. Sign a lease and protect yourself prior to putting your business on the market.

How long has your business been at this location?

This answer too will determine if you can relocate your business or not. Is your business relocatable? If so, how far can it be moved? If your business can be relocated anywhere in the USA, then we will have a much larger buying pool. Relocatable businesses sell like hotcakes and we can't keep them on the shelves!

Do you operate your business out of your home?

There are many home-based businesses these days that do very well and generate great profits. These types of businesses are great to sell because there is no lease involved and they are relocatable. Buyers are intrigued and interested in being able to run and operate their business from home. This way they can have the best of both worlds: a great home-based business and they get to spend more time with their family. Some businesses are operated in an office space that is a separate building on the owner's land, which is typically close to the owner's home. This could be a good option for the buyer as long as the seller is willing to sell the building and the land that it sits on, or lease the building to the buyer. Either option can work for both parties. Sometimes the owner is willing to sell the office building on the land along with their home. This too is a good option for a buyer, especially out-of-state buyers.

Do you own the real estate?

Owning the real estate is a huge benefit for sellers. It provides you with a lot more options to offer buyers. In addition, owning the real estate will enlarge your buyer pool, and more people will be interested in looking at your business and the real estate. It also provides you with more

> It's amazing to me how many sellers do not want to invest in getting their land/building appraised.

versatility. You can sell the building, lease to purchase, or simply lease the space to the buyer who is purchasing your business. You can also sell the building to someone completely different than the buyer of your business. If your building is located on prime real estate, especially a corner location, then that opens up even more possibilities for larger type tenants, such as drug store, fast food chains, or drive-up dry cleaners. The possibilities are endless, especially if the business is relocatable; then you can capitalize on selling both. If you own the real estate, then you should have an appraisal. If you do not have an appraisal, then obtain one as soon as possible. If your appraisal is old, then obtain a recent appraisal. It's amazing to me how many sellers do not want to invest in getting their land/building appraised.

Spend the money! It will only cost $1,000-$3,000 in most cases. It's worth the investment. Otherwise you really do not know what your property is worth. Sure we can run comps; however, sometimes there are no comps in your particular area and a lot of times the comps may not be accurate. Ask for referrals and hire a competent appraisal firm to appraise your property. Trust me; in the end it will be worth it and it will aid in maximizing your value. It is also important to know what you owe on your property. Some owners are upside down in debt on their property and business, and they cannot afford to sell for enough money to pay off their debts.

Owning the real estate also provides you with added security when selling your business and helps secure seller financing. I sold a company where the business was listed for $560,000 and the real estate was listed for $390,000. The buyer needed seller financing. They could put up forty percent of the entire transaction; however, they wanted the deposit to pay off the building and the remaining deposit to go towards the business. The seller was having to owner finance the majority of the business. There were five things we put in place to secure seller financing and ensure our seller gets paid. One thing we did was insist that the seller would have a mortgage on the building. No mortgage no deal. This way the seller could foreclose on the building and have additional recourses that we secured the financing with.

Leasing Your Property

If you are going to lease your property, then you need to know a few things and do research on the following items listed below.

What are your mortgage, property taxes, and insurance?

Hopefully you know your square footage. You need to know what the rents are going for in your community. Will you do a straight lease or a triple net? A triple net lease means the lessee pays the rent, property taxes, and insurance. You cannot come up with rental rates and terms unless you are clear on your expenses. I have seen business owners charge the buyer of their business less on the lease of their property than what they are paying on their mortgage, property taxes, and insurances. You will also have to decide on how long a lease, and how many options and rental increases you are willing to offer. Remember, it has to be in line with other comparables and it has to make sense to the buyer. Otherwise, you may lose on the sale of your business if you do not offer favorable terms on your property lease. Leasing your property is another way to secure seller financing. You should tie the lease to the seller financing payments. If the buyer of the business does not pay their payments, then you will have the right to evict them and take over the business.

In summary, know if you have brand loyalty or location loyalty before selling your business. If your business is based upon location loyalty rather than brand loyalty, then you may want to consider hiring a professional to assist you in building your brand before or during the selling process. My firm provides consulting/mentoring services to assist our sellers in improving their business in order to sell their business for maximum value.

 For **MENTORING AND CONSULTING SERVICES AND TO RECEIVE A FREE CONSULTATION,** visit www.betterbusinessbrokers.com
(877) 853-4227

As mentioned above, do your research ahead of time or align yourself with a professional, experienced business broker that can assist you with selling your brand or your location or both.

CHAPTER SIX

Are You Selling
a Business or a Job?

SO MANY BUSINESS OWNERS TRULY BELIEVE THEY HAVE A BUSINESS TO SELL. There is a tremendous number of business owners that don't really own a business, they own a glorified job and the business owns them. As you are reading this chapter, you are probably starting to get a little hot under the collar. I don't blame you, I would too. I have owned eight different businesses in my career. I have owned my business brokerage firm for years, and now I own a business brokerage franchise with several offices throughout the United States. I thought I owned a pretty good business; then one day JT Foxx, real estate investor, entrepreneur, mentor and speaker, said to me in front of hundreds of people, "Michelle you don't own a business, you own a glorified job!" JT has a way of calling it as it is. Like many people, I could have become defensive, but I didn't. I asked him what he meant. He asked, "Can you walk away from your business for months at a time and focus on growing your company and other businesses and your business still maintains its success?" I said no. He asked, "Can you take extensive vacations without penalty?" I responded with a big, fat NO. He asked, "Who runs the business when you are not there, who is in charge to make daily decisions, who is in charge to put out fires? Who hires and fires employees in your firm? Do you have a sales manager, an operations manager, anyone in charge other than you?" As JT continued to ask me these questions, my Business Bubble was beginning to burst! However, I did not get defensive or upset, because I knew he was right. I had to make some serious changes in my own company so I too could maximize value when I sell my company one day. I had agents and an administrative staff. However, what I realized is that I was not delegating enough. I was selling businesses that my agents should have been selling, and I was making absolutely every single decision. My philosophy was "If you want it done right then you have to do it yourself." And that is true to some extent, but you will never grow your businesses to the next level with that mentality. Since then, I have let go of control and I have made a lot of prudent changes that will ensure that my business can run and flourish without me. I'm implementing policies, procedures, and protocols so my business works for me; I don't work for my business. Now keep in mind that I still oversee my business. I inspect what I expect from my agents, employees, office owners, and clients. Some of you will want to implement changes as well before you market your business for sale.

For a **SAMPLE OF AN OPERATIONS MANUAL,** visit
www.betterbusinessbrokers.com
(877) 853-4227

Now, with that being said, there are different types of businesses that buyers are attracted to, which I will explain in greater detail. It is important to know what category your business falls in and/or what category you want your business to fall in before you market your business for sale.

One Man/One Woman Show/Business

The first type of business is what I call the one man/woman show/business: These are businesses that are a hundred percent dependent on the owner being there. If you take the owner out of the equation, then you have nothing to sell. The owner is the business! Some examples are as follows:

- Real estate brokerage firm with few to no agents
- Plumbing business where the owner works out of his/her house and has no employees. They utilize independent contractors as needed.
- AC & Heating business where the owner works out of his/her house and has no employees. They utilize independent contractors as needed.
- Construction business where the owner works out of his/her house and has no employees. They utilize independent contractors when need be.
- Appraisal business. They typically have few to no employees, and some work out of their home.
- Janitorial business where the owner works out of his/ her home and has few to no employees. They utilize independent contractors as needed.
- Travel agents typically have few to no employees, and some work out of their home.
- Engineers are a skilled profession; however, most engineering firms consist of the engineer and administrative staff. If you take that engineer out of the business, then you really have nothing to sell.
- Interior decorator business: the decorator typically has one to two employees or independent contractors and usually works out of their home or a small shop. The decorator is licensed and has skill sets that are not easily duplicable. You take the decorator out of the business, what do

you have? Most decorators will start their own business or purchase a business with many employees and a healthy customer base.

- Doctors, chiropractors, and dentists are another perfect example of a business that are difficult to sell (but not impossible) because number one, they are licensed profession, and number two, they are relationship businesses dependent on that particular doctor, chiropractor, or dentist. These medical businesses are sellable, especially if they employ other doctors, chiropractors, and dentists that work in the business. That way the business is not solely dependent on the physician/business owner. It is very difficult to sell sole practitioner businesses due to the fact that once the physician leaves it is very likely that the patients will leave as well.

These are just a few examples. There are certainly more examples that I could provide; however, I think you get the gist. So the question to you should be: Do these types of businesses sell? My answer is that it depends; as with any business, some sell, some don't. It all depends if the business/job is priced right. If the business/job is overpriced, then a buyer will look at the business to determine if he/she can start the business on their own for less. In the previous chapters I talked about buyers. There are millions unemployed who need to replace their income! They are looking to buy a job or a small business. It also depends if the small business/job needs special skill sets and licenses such as HVAC companies, plumbing, real estate agency, appraisal companies, and more. If an individual is a licensed plumber or AC & Heating technician, then that individual will probably start their own business or buy a larger business with a location, employees, FF&E, and most important, they will buy a business with more cash flow. If a person has his/her real estate broker's license, then they will start their own firm, hang their license with a firm, or buy a firm with listings and agents. The real estate broker in all likelihood will not buy a one man/woman show. However, there are always exceptions to the rule. I sold an appraisal business/job. This business/job had one owner and no employees and operated from home. He was making decent money. I had a buyer who wanted to get into an appraisal business. My buyer did not have any experience nor did he have an appraisal license, which is required. In the appraisal industry in the state of Louisiana, you have to go to school and work under someone's license for two years. The licensed person has to sign off on all your appraisals for two years. Therefore, my seller had no other choice than to sell to an existing appraiser or sell to a non-licensed appraiser. An existing appraiser did not want to pay my seller what his business was worth. The non-licensed buyer was happy to pay list price if the seller agreed to stay on for two years to sign off on all his appraisals. I negotiated the deal based upon list price with fifty percent down and fifty percent seller financing to ensure the buyer that the seller would stay the two years needed. My firm lists/sells small business/jobs all day long if the business/job is salable. If I don't think we can sell them, then we simply don't list them.

Small Business Owners

These businesses are small cafes, coffee shops, restaurants, bars, convenience stores, dry cleaners, clothing stores, gift shops, day cares, and more. They are businesses that don't depend on the owner a hundred percent. These businesses will typically have three to seven employees. The consumer is more concerned with good service and quality. They don't necessarily have to deal directly with the owner. However, if the owner is not involved heavily in the business, then the business will not be successful for a multitude of reasons. Small business owners have to be careful of theft, employees not showing up, lack of customer service, and more. Like the old saying goes, "No one is going to run/care about your business like you run/care about your business."

Absentee Business

The absentee businesses are great businesses to sell. However, I have news for you; there is no such thing as a complete absentee business. These businesses still require some owner hands-on, but not near as much as other businesses. These businesses are your Laundromats, storage facilities, some car washes, trailer parks, apartment complexes, to name a few. These businesses sell quicker than all other businesses. The reason is that because there are a lot more buyers that want to invest their money and receive residual income without a lot of effort. There are a lot of hands-off buyers looking for these treasures. If the business cash flows, then I can always maximize value and sell these businesses quickly. They don't all show positive cash flow, and that makes it very difficult to sell them. The issues are that a lot of these particular business owners do not report their cash, which makes it nearly impossible to maximize value. We will talk about hidden income in Chapter 7: Report all Your Income or Lose Huge Profits in the Sale of Your Business.

Small to Medium Size Companies

These companies usually have 5-10 employees. They typically gross a million and up. They usually will have a manager in place; however, the owner is still involved. These are good businesses to sell. They are in different industries than your typical small business. Some of these industries are distribution, manufacturing, wholesale, some retail, education, and the service industry. These types of businesses are attractive to buyers. Many buyers are looking for a stable business that is making a profit with employees in place.

Middle Market or M&A (Mergers & Acquisitions) Companies

Most of these companies have been in business for years; they have anywhere from 15 to hundreds of employees. They have management in place. The larger companies will typically have a CEO, CFO, and an Operations Manager. They will have tenured employees in place. They will have a significant client base with revenues in the millions. Depending upon the business, the owner may not be as involved as the previous types of businesses mentioned because they own a business, not a job, and they have good quality employees in place. These businesses are also very desirable to buyers. The only issue is that the buyer pool will be smaller due to the fact that not everyone can afford this type of business. However, rest assured there are buyers for these businesses. We have hundreds of buyers in our database searching for these types of companies. In addition, my firms work with over twenty five hundred private equity firms looking for these businesses on a daily basis.

We discussed five types of businesses for sale and the different buyers for each. Which type of category does your business fit in? Below are some additional questions I ask my sellers when evaluating and selling their business. In order to maximize your value, you might want to ask yourself the same questions.

- I always ask my larger companies if they have an organizational chart.
- How many employees do you have?
  - What is their average education level?
  - What is their skill level?
  - What is your employee retention rate?
  - What is your employee average tenure?
  - Is it difficult to find skilled employees for your business?
  - How many employees do you replace a year?

- What employment agreements do you have in place?
- Do you have any non-compete agreements with employees?
- What is your average compensation plan and employee benefit program that you offer?

- What is your recruiting method?
- How much money do you spend on training in a year?
- Do you have an in-house human resource department?
- Can your business run without you?
- Do you have a management team in place? Will they assist with the transfer?
- Do you have a CFO or an in-house bookkeeper?

If you are able to answer yes to the majority of those questions, then you have a sizeable business that should be evaluated by a professional, experienced business broker in order to sell your business for maximum value. If not and you have a smaller business, then rest assured that your business could still be salable. Again, there are many buyers looking to acquire small businesses generating profits. My firm has a good mix of small, medium, and larger size companies for sale at any given time.

CHAPTER SEVEN

Report All Your Income or Lose Huge Profits in the Sale of Your Business

THUS FAR WE HAVE TALKED ABOUT DIFFERENT TYPES OF BUSINESSES AND DIFferent types of buyers. We have discussed a multitude of things that will make your business sell for more than other businesses. This chapter is where the rubber meets the road. This is where a majority of small businesses fall short.

Let's face it; being in business for yourself is an everyday battle. It is a battle just to open your doors. Every day we have to deal with customers, employees, vendors, landlords, lenders, and so much more. Most importantly, it is a huge battle to deal with our not so favorite uncle: Uncle Sam!

Uncle Sam makes it very difficult for small business owners to make a profit. By the time they pay for cost of goods, employees, and all the other expenses, there is not much left over for the owner who breaks their back every day trying to run their business in these difficult times we live in.

- There are over twenty seven million businesses in the USA and 99.9 percent are small business owners (firms

with fewer than 500 employees) according to the United States Census Bureau.

- Small business owners cannot afford to stay in business if they don't realize a profit to take care of their family and their living expenses.

- The majority of small business owners do not take a salary. They cannot afford to take a salary because they have to pay even more taxes on their salary.

- The majority of small, medium sized, and some larger business owners will run personal expenses through their business to decrease their tax liability. Some common things that business owners run through their business are listed below:

  - Auto
  - Travel
  - Car Insurance
  - Gas for all family members' cars
  - Health Insurance
  - Retirement Fund
  - Home Remodeling
  - Meals
  - Entertainment
  - Phone
  - Donations

- I have seen it all. There are a lot more personal expenses that business owners run through their business. This is not a tell-all book; therefore, I'm going to stick to the above list. However, I will tell you that boys love their toys and women love to shop till they drop and a lot of this spending is run through the business.

- The bigger issue becomes when a seller is trying to sell their business; they really don't know what their business is worth. Simply because the seller, in most cases, does not take a salary and they have been running personal expenses through the business for so long that they actually do not know what they really make at the end of the day. Think about it; if you have been running personal expenses through your business for years, it will be very difficult to remember exactly what you ran through the business – and can you prove it?

- When I work with my sellers, I add any and all personal expenses back to the bottom line when evaluating what their business is worth. However, the seller must be able to prove what they are running through the business. If they cannot prove their personal expenses to a buyer, than I will not add it back. I walk my sellers through this painful process line item by line item. It's amusing to me when my sellers tell me to take their tax returns and P&L statements and add back what I think. What am I, a psychic? I don't have a crystal ball; I can't predict the future. It has to be up to my seller to tell me and my agents exactly what they are running though their business. Of course, there are common items that always get added back. Such as:
  - Depreciation
  - Amortization
  - Interest (sometimes)
  - Owner's salary (sometimes)
  - Rent (only if the sellers owns the real estate and their company pays their real estate holding company rent.)

Please keep in mind that there are always exceptions to the rule. Interest and owner's salary are typically added back, but it is not a definite add back. Let's take into consideration owner's salary. We usually always add back the owner's salary. However, if a buyer is buying a business and he/she is not going to run the business, then we don't add back the owner's salary because the buyer is hiring someone to do the owner's job. But, if the owner is taking $50,000 a year and the average manager's salary for that position is $30,000, then we would add back $20,000. If there is a husband and wife team and/or partners who both work,

> Buyers want to know and understand what you are truly making in your business.

and they pay themselves a $100,000 annually, you cannot assume that the $100,000 is an add back. In all likelihood, the buyer will not be able to perform the task of both husband and wife or partners. Therefore, we will add back only the difference in what it would take to replace one person based on their skill sets. There are resources my firm utilizes to determine average salaries for all types of different positions around the United States. There are business owners that will pay family members through the business; however, that family member does not actually work in the business. This will be an add back as long as the family member does not contribute to the business.

Interest is typically an add back. However, not always; it depends on the business. If you own a car dealership, boat dealership, motorcycle dealership, or anything with a floor plan, then you cannot simply add back interest. In a floor plan business, interest is a legitimate expense that will be carried over to the new owner.

If you own the real estate in a separate corporation and are paying that corporation excess rent over and above comparable to what you would charge your tenant, then you can only add back the difference. For example, I have a seller that pays her separate corporation $250,000 a year in rent. If the new owner cannot afford to buy the building, then she will rent the space to them for $150,000 a year; therefore, we are only adding back $100,000 yearly. If a buyer is going to buy the building, then the buyer is buying and building equity, and in that case we will add back the entire $250,000.

If your business does not show a healthy profit on its tax returns, then it is almost impossible to sell the business without going through this exercise.

Here is another example: I had a listing appointment with a seller who owned three car and truck accessory retail stores. The owner was adamant about selling his business for a million dollars. The seller did not want to sell unless we could sell his business for a million dollars. When I looked at his tax returns, he was losing money in 2008, and he made a whopping profit of $8,500 in 2009. Based upon his tax returns, there was no way I could sell his business for a million dollars. He had approximately $300,000 in inventory and he owned the real estate, but he was not selling the real estate. He had very little in FF&E. The seller was adamant that he was making lots of money and he had lots of boy toys. He was not even taking a salary. In order to maximize his value, I had to dig deep. I had to peel back all the layers of the onion (his financials) to see what his true SDE (seller's discretionary earnings) really was. It took me four months to literally go through all his books and records. At the end of the day, he was not losing money; to the contrary, he was profiting close to $400,000 annually and we could prove it. On average, I am able to sell my client's business for twenty to forty percent more than they could ever sell it for on their own. I did not sell his business for the million dollars he so desperately wanted! I sold his business for $1,200,000 in 30 days.

There is yet another problem that will occur when you run personal expenses through the businesses; i.e., lending. No lender would have taken this deal or any deal that looked like it. Lenders will account for some add backs, but not to that extent. My seller had to agree to hold paper on fifty percent of the transaction. That is the only way his business would have sold. However, it was a great deal for him. He received $600,000 upfront and seven percent interest on his money for five years. He also was able to keep the real estate and lease all three buildings to the buyer for a profit. He was also able to utilize his leases as additional security on the seller financing portion.

Above are just a few examples of add backs. This can get very complicated, and it is very difficult to accomplish on your own. Many business owners have sloppy books and records. Again, this is a difficult process to navigate on your own. You can truly maximize your value if you utilize the assistance of a professional, experienced business broker to peel back all the layers of the onion in order to uncover what the SDE (seller's discretionary earnings) really is. Without identifying the SDE, you really do not know what your business is truly worth.

Some business owners have a cash component in their business. This is where the rubber meets the road, yet again. If you are not reporting your cash, then you cannot get paid for your cash from a buyer. This is crazy to me! I tell my sellers all the time to report their cash. You might save approximately fifteen to twenty percent paying taxes yearly by not reporting your cash. However, it is illegal and there are consequences. In addition, the fifteen to twenty percent you save in hiding cash will cost you significantly when selling your business. If I can sell your business for a multiple of earnings, then the return on the sale of your business far exceeds the small amount that you are saving in not paying in taxes.

Pricing your business will heavily depend on a multitude of your business's characteristics. However, in reality it always comes down to brass tacks; buyers want to know and understand what you are truly making in your business.

To **DOWNLOAD A FINANCIAL SPREADSHEET TEMPLATE,** visit
www.betterbusinessbrokers.com
(877) 853-4227

CHAPTER EIGHT

The Key Elements to Determining What Your Business is Really Worth and Selling it for More

IF YOU ARE TRULY INTERESTED IN SELLING YOUR BUSINESS, THEN IT'S TIME TO clean your financial house. You are going to have to provide financial records to the buyer and lender. As mentioned in the previous chapter, you are going to have to decipher what you are making in your business in order to price your business. Again, I would consult with an expert to assist you in navigating through the process. Below are all the forms that you will need to provide to the buyer, the buyer's CPA, and perhaps their lender. If you hire a business broker, then you need to provide these documents to the business broker; the broker will then distribute documents as needed to the buyer and their professional team. However, my firm will put together an offering memorandum that includes a three-to five-year financial spread-sheet highlighting the add backs. We will not give our seller's tax returns and other proprietary documents to buyers and their team without a written and executed purchase offer contract with escrow money.

Seller must provide 3-5 years of the following:

- Tax Returns
- Profit and Loss Statements
- Current Balance Sheet
- W-2s

Additional Items:

- AR Report
- AP Report
- FF&E List
- Inventory
- Appraisal if applicable
- Lease if applicable

Seller must be able to prove what he/she is running through the business

We talked about this in great detail in the previous chapter. Please refer to the list of common add backs and not so common add backs.

Seller must provide a current FF&E list

Sometimes this list is attached to the tax returns as a depreciated schedule and sometimes it is not. It is imperative to have or put together a complete list of your furniture, fixtures, and equipment. In some cases, especially large manufacturing companies and large construction companies, these companies may have to obtain an FF&E appraisal. The FF&E list is sometimes my firm's worst nightmare. This list becomes the Bible and it is attached to the closing documents. Sellers are constantly changing things, throwing things away, replacing equipment, and/or adding new furniture, fixtures, and equipment. Typically, something will break and the seller needs to replace it, and/or the franchisor requires the seller to purchase new equipment or signage. It is imperative that when you change, replace, or throw away any furniture, fixtures, or equipment that you also change your list and/or notify your broker to do so. The buyer has the right to walk through your business two to three days prior to closing and inspect all FF&E on the list. If something is broken, then you need to fix it or replace it before the closing. If something is missing and has not been replaced, then you need to replace it before closing or make concessions for the buyer.

Sellers must provide an inventory report and/or count

We typically do not need an inventory report. However, all inventory is included in the sale of the business at cost, not retail. At closing, inventory is usually adjusted upward or downward. There are some businesses that have massive inventory, and that inventory report is critical to pricing the business. Example: I have a company that specializes in oil field rental, sale, and service. Their inventory is valued for several millions. This inventory is an intricate part of their business and in most cases this inventory stays with the company for ongoing rentals to their clients. This inventory has to be listed and valued by a professional inventory company in order to maximize value. Keep in mind that the buyer will walk through your business one to three days before closing to take an inventory count. This is done in a multitude of ways. If it is a small business, then the buyer and seller agree to take inventory together. Medium size to larger companies may require the assistance of a third-party inventory company. This fee is usually split between buyer and seller.

Sellers must provide an AR report (Accounts Receivable)

Most small businesses will not have accounts receivables. However, medium sized to large businesses will. It is important to know what the average AR runs monthly and what the typical collection rate is. We usually assign a price tag and include AR in the total value of the company. This is a point of negotiations for buyers. Some buyers will not buy the business without the AR, and some will not pay for the AR because they feel they won't able to collect.

AP Report (Accounts Payable and debt owed on the business)

It's important for a broker to know what is owed on the business and/or real estate. There are two types of sales: Asset Sale and Stock Sale. We will discuss both later in the book. If a buyer is buying your business, which includes intellectual property, cash flow, FF&E, and inventory, then the seller will need to pay off any loans, leases, or accounts payable on the FF&E and inventory. The attorney will do a title search to make sure there are no liens on the furniture, fixtures, and equipment. If so, the debt will have to be paid off, and the lien will need to be removed prior to closing or out of the closing escrow account. If a buyer is buying the business and it is a stock sale, then the buyer will receive the stock, inventory, FF&E, cash on hand, all Accounts Receivables and Payables. Many sellers feel that if the buyer retains the Accounts Receivables, then the buyer should be responsible for the Accounts Payables as well. That is not always correct. It depends on an Asset versus Stock sale and it depends on the business. Sometimes the buyer and seller will implement a cutoff date for AR and AP upon closing. This can become complicated; again, it's imperative that you utilize a professional to navigate through all the legalities.

Sellers must provide a copy of the lease

The broker/buyer needs to see your lease. We spoke about leases in Chapter Five. Make sure you have a solid lease. If you have a month-to-month lease, then buyers can and will go behind your back and negotiate with the landlord on your space. Buyers are not always interested in buying an existing business. Some of them are really more interested in your location. As I mentioned earlier in the book, it's crazy to start a new business versus buying an existing business; however, there are crazy people out there. It is very beneficial if your lease is transferable or if you can sublease.

Provide a copy of real estate appraisal if there is one

You need to have a recent real estate appraisal; if not, obtain one. This small investment will pay off immensely in the sale of your business.

Evaluating what a business is worth

There is no one size that fits all when evaluating what a business is worth. I certainly do not want to point fingers at any one profession. However, CPAs frighten me when it comes to valuating businesses. My sellers have told me about insane stories of what their CPA said their business is worth. I have heard different formulas that make absolutely no sense, such as five times gross income. No one is going to pay you five times gross for your business. It does not make sense! I have also had sellers that were very upset because their CPA charged them $15,000-$20,000 to valuate their business. Sellers engage my firm to sell their business for the amount that the CPA valuated their business for. However, my firm has to start from scratch and re-valuate the seller's business, because in most cases the seller's CPA valuated their business for way too much, or sometimes the valuation was way too low. I listed a physical therapy business for sale a year ago. The partners had paid their CPA $17,000 dollars to valuate their business. He valuated their business for close to $600,000. He did not pull industry standards. He did not pull business comps. He did not back into the cash flow to see if the business cash flows enough to support a $600,000 asking price. When I take listings I don't price the businesses based upon the CPA's valuation or another business broker's valuation or what the seller wants for their business. I run the numbers, I pull industry standards, and I pull business comps. I also look at all the other characteristics of the business before pricing the business. Therefore, I valuated the physical therapy business. I did not come up with a price tag of $600,000. That number did not compute. They had only been in business for three years and were making a little over $100,000 a year with add backs. Upon completing my valuation, I told them that their business was worth $430,000. Needless to say they were shocked, devastated, and upset that my valuation was so far off from their CPA's valuation. Therefore, I showed them the facts. I showed them industry standards, business comps, and most important, I backed into their cash flow and demonstrated how the cash flow will not meet the buyer's debt service, will not leave the buyer with enough money to live on, and not give the buyer a return on their investment for years to come, if ever. I told them the $600,000 price tag will not meet the buyer's sanity check and no one will buy. When I explained my valuation to the partners, they completely understood and were furious that they paid their CPA $17,000 to give them an unsalable price on their business. I listed their business for $430,000 and received an offer for $460,000. I was able to sell their business for the highest maximum value in 30 days.

Businesses are valuated on percentages
or a multiple of the following:

- **Gross Income:** This is the total gross income of your business. However, you should not consider non-related business income to be included in your gross income. Such as other rental income that is not included in the sale of your business, insurance claims related to storms or the BP oil spill. This income is not the norm and should not be utilized in the valuations of your business.

- **EBITDA** (Earnings before interest, taxes, depreciation, and amortization)

- **EBIT** (Earnings before interest and taxes)

- **SDE** (Seller's Discretionary Earnings)

- **Net Income** (net income or loss that appears on your tax returns)

Again there is not one size that fits all. Many industries utilize several formulas to determine the selling price. My firm evaluates each formula associated with industry standards to determine which formula will maximize the value of your business.

To **OBTAIN INDUSTRY STANDARDS FOR YOUR PARTICULAR INDUSTRY,** visit
www.betterbusinessbrokers.com
(877) 853-4227

Allocating a Price Tag on Your Business

When allocating a price tag on your business you must take into consideration the items listed below. I wrote in great detail regarding each of these in previous chapters.

- **Industry:** Is your industry unique? Are buyers attracted to it? Will your industry demand top dollar?

- **Location:** Is your business based upon brand loyalty or location loyalty?

- **Years in Business:** The longer in business the greater the return.

- **Trademarks/Trade Secrets:** These are valuable commodities that buyers will pay top dollar for.

- **Customer Contracts in Place:** This adds tremendous value to the price of your business, especially if the contracts are transferable.

- **Business Trend:** If your business is trending up every year, then you can typically obtain a higher sales price. If your business is trending down every year, then it could lower the price of your business, depending on the reasons your business is trending downward.

- **FF&E:** FF&E certainly adds value to the price of your business. However, if you are upside down in FF&E, and the cash flow does not support the price tag on your furniture, fixtures, and equipment, then you might not be able to recoup your investment on your FF&E. I went on a listing appointment for a manufacturing company last year. The sellers wanted $1,200,000 for their business because their FF&E and inventory was valued over a million. Their cash flow was only $40,000-50,000 per year. They were upside down in FF&E and inventory. The cash flow does not come anywhere close to supporting the asking price. My sellers did not understand that. They put the business on the market and have not had one inquiry since. They will not sell at that price unless they improve their cash flow.

- **Inventory:** Inventory adds value to your business as well as increases the selling price. However, the same thing is true for inventory as with FF&E. If you are upside down in inventory and the cash flow of your business does not support the investment in inventory, then you may have to take a loss on your inventory or seller finance your inventory.

- **AR** (Accounts Receivables): We mentioned AR earlier in this chapter. Accounts Receivables will add value and increase your selling price if you have a solid track record of collecting at least ninety percent of your receivables.

- **Working Capital:** Some owners will include the cash on hand or in the bank, so to speak. If you have $100,000 for working capital in the bank and you want to include it, then you will get paid for it. Again, cash on hand/working capital can be a negotiating tool. I have a supply company under contract to close. The buyer is borrowing the money from his retirement fund and will not have enough money for working capital. Therefore, I encouraged the seller to leave $30,000 in the bank for working capital, and increase the sales price by $30,000, and seller finance it to the buyer. This way everyone wins. The seller gets paid for the working capital plus seven percent interest on his working capital, and the buyer will be set up for success and not failure by having enough money to continue to run the company.

- **Real Estate:** Real Estate always adds value to the purchase price. However, if the cash flow of the business does not support the asking price of the real estate, then in all likelihood the buyer will not be able to afford to purchase the real estate, and you will have to rent the space to the new buyer. Or you can sell the real estate to another buyer other than the buyer purchasing the business.

- **AND MORE:** There are always components in a business that add value or take away value. I obviously cannot cover them all in this book, but when evaluating a business for sale I absolutely take everything into consideration. So I can, in most cases, sell my client's business for more than it is worth in the quickest amount of time possible!

The items listed above should and will be considered in pricing your business for sale. Some business owners have unrealistic expectations, while others way undervalue their business. Which seller are you?

In closing, the most important thing you need to know is the price of the business must meet the Buyer Sanity Check or no one will buy and your business will sit on the market for years and perhaps never sell.

The Buyer Sanity Check includes five questions that buyers ask themselves before making an offer.

- How much money do I have to put down on this business?
- Will the cash flow of the business cover the debt service?
- After debt service is paid, how much money is left for me to live on?
- How soon can I get a return on my initial deposit?
- Does the business have potential to grow? Buyers will not pay for potential; however, they will not buy a business unless it has potential to grow. Buyers are not going to pay twice! It takes money, time, energy, and effort to grow a business to the next level. Buyers are not going to pay a seller for potential that could be and then have to pay more money to actually realize the potential.

Most buyers will not buy a business if they cannot receive positive answers to the questions listed above. In addition, most buyers want to recoup their initial deposit within two-three years.

Therefore, if the price tag on your business does not line up with the Buyer Sanity Check, then your price does not make sense and will not appeal to buyers. When selling your business, ask yourself this question: Do you want a high price for your business and your business does not support your asking price? Or do you want your business to sell? There are thousands of overpriced businesses that have been sitting on the market for years and will never sell because they are overpriced. You need to be very selective when choosing a business broker to handle the sale of your business. I have a seller that called me up one day and wanted me to valuate his business. He was listed with my competitor for three years at $7,000,000. I asked the seller who came up with that price tag, him or the broker? The seller replied, "I did." I then asked the seller if the broker performed a valuation and pulled industry standards and business comps. He replied, "NO!" I pulled up his listing and discovered that the business had been reduced to $5,000,000. I then asked him if the business broker valuated his company to come up with a more realistic price or if something changed in his business to lower the price by $2,000,000. He replied "Nothing changed to lower my price by $2,000,000. I just was not getting any interested buyers; therefore, I called the broker and had him lower the price." The broker was merely an order taker, not a professional business broker. Unfortunately, you cannot blame it on lack of experience because he has been in business brokering for many years. However, he did nothing whatsoever to valuate and sell the seller's business.

I met with the seller and performed an extensive valuation on his business. His business was not worth anywhere close to $7,000,000 or even $5,000,000. It was worth $3,800,000. We are now in the process of reviewing offers in the $4,200,000 range. As mentioned many times, I can typically obtain a 20-40 percent higher selling price than my seller's business appraises for. I had to ask my seller a very important question: Do you want a high price for your business or do you want it to sell for maximum value in the quickest time possible? The seller is in his seventies and wants to maximize value in the shortest time possible. There is a big difference between hiring a professional, experienced business broker and an order taker. Please pay close attention to Chapter Twenty and make sure you properly interview and hire an experienced business broker, not an order taker. Your business is too valuable to leave to chance!

The key is to price and package your business correctly so it will sell in the quickest amount of time possible for the maximum value.

For **ASSISTANCE ON PRICING YOUR BUSINESS,** visit
www.betterbusinessbrokers.com
(877) 853-4227

CHAPTER NINE

Minimize Clutter and Make Your Business Appear Better

IN MOST CASES, SELLING YOUR BUSINESS WILL BE THE MOST IMPORTANT DECISION you will ever make and will be the most valuable thing you will ever sell in your lifetime. Therefore, in order to obtain maximum value, you are going to have to roll up your sleeves, get dirty, and use some elbow grease. We discussed financial housekeeping in the previous chapter. In some cases, buyers will see the financials and marketing materials before they actually visit your business. In other situations, buyers will look at the business first before reviewing financials. Either way, it is imperative that you clean your business from top to bottom, inside and out. When selling a house, you or your real estate agent will usually stage the house for sale. They will tell you to start with the outside and work your way in. Buyers will judge your house/business by what they see on the outside way before walking in to your house/business. Realtors will tell you to spruce up and clean the entire outside and remove clutter and oversized furniture on the inside. Less is more when you are showing a house. The same holds true for a business. Granted, you do not have to go through the same extent you would when staging a house for sale. You are not going to redo cabinets, flooring, and decorate the place so it looks like no one lives/works there.

However, you will have to look at your business and its surroundings through the eyes of a buyer.

When buyers meet you or the business broker at your business, they are going to judge your location, visibility signage, and curb appeal. They are going to judge if they think the business is busy or slow, if they think the owner runs a tight ship, if the employees are dressed professionally, staff is courteous, and so on.

It is obviously easier to stage a house versus a business. Let's face it; we seem to live in our business more than our home. In addition, the employees do not (should not) know the business is for sale, so it's not like you can now tell them to start wearing uniforms, etc. However, you should enlist the employees to help you clean up shop. They do not need to know you are selling in order to clean up the business and remove clutter.

Over the years of selling businesses, I have seen it all. I have walked into businesses that were so filthy, dusty, and full of animal hair that I could not breathe. I literally had to meet my sellers outside or have them come to my office. If I cannot walk in, because I get sick from the dust and the animal hair, what do you think a buyer is going to do? They too will have to walk in and walk out without any further consideration of buying the business. There are a lot of businesses on the market today. It is a very competitive industry; when you put your business on the market you are competing with all other businesses and franchises for sale. If you want to maximize value when selling your business, then you need to make your business shine above all others.

Not too long ago I went to list a B&B (Bread and Breakfast) for sale. It was a fantastic location, quaint and very charming. My sellers had canceled our listing meeting four times because they were always sick. I could not for the life of me figure out what was wrong with them. Finally, one day they decided to stick to their schedule and meet with me. The minute I walked in, I then realized why they were always so sick. This B&B should have been on the show *Hoarders*! The sellers had everything you could imagine in their business. Everything was stacked from floor to ceiling. Everything was filthy and dusty. They were sick from allergies caused from all the clutter and dust mites. It was a beautiful, charming B&B; however, I could not show it to my buyers because you barely could see the walls, floors, or ceilings. I asked the sellers to go through every room and decide what is staying and what is going. I recommended that they remove about fifty percent of all the furnishings, decorations, antiques, and plain junk. They said they would, but of course they have not. I have showed the business to prospective buyers numerous times; however, the potential buyers just can't seem to get past the obvious clutter to realize the potential of this quaint, charming B&B.

> When buyers meet you or the business broker at your business, they are going to judge your location, visibility signage, and curb appeal.

Do not be lazy when selling your business! Do whatever it takes to earn your big payday. I listed the B&B for $1,400,000, including the real estate, but not the trash. Till this day they have not lifted one finger to clean house, and to this day they are still always sick! I guess it's a catch-22; they can't clean due to their health, and they can't get healthy due to living in filth. I stopped bringing buyers to see the property until they take control of their business/life and hire a cleaning/trash removal company to remove the clutter to make their B&B look better.

The areas below are key elements that buyers will look at and use to form their own perception. Buyer's perception becomes your reality. Be proactive and create positive perceptions. If you are going to lose a buyer, let's not lose them over how the business looks. The better your business looks on the outside will provide buyers with peace of mind that if you can maintain cleanliness on the outside, then you must be properly managing the business, and the financials must be clean as well. Let's face it; we live in a very judgmental society. Everyone judges everything. I can assure you that if you follow the tips in this book, then you will only leave buyers with the perception of wanting to know more, see more, and most important, pay more.

Below are areas you should focus on before you put your business on the market.

Curb Appeal

- Make sure the parking lot is clean. This is an important, cost-effective and easy thing to do, and boy, does it make a difference. When buyers drive up to your parking lot, it is one of the first things they see. If your parking lot is dirty and filled with trash, then they have already formed a negative opinion before even walking into the business.

- Make sure the sidewalk is clean. The sidewalk is one of the next things buyers look at. Again, it sets the stage for what's inside. If the parking lot and curb looks spick and span, then buyers will walk into the business with a very positive attitude before they even open the door.

- Make sure the door is clean. I know this all sounds like common sense; however, common sense is not as common as it once was. If the parking lot is clean and the curb is clean but the door is dirty or it has ugly decals stuck all over it, then the buyer's perception has just changed from positive to negative that quickly before opening the door. Make sure the door and glass in the door is very clean. Paint the door if need be. Hang a new Open and Closed sign if need be. These are all very inexpensive fixes that will earn you money at the closing table.

- Make sure the windows are clean. The windows are as important as the door. Many of us are window shoppers and we like to take a sneak peek before we walk in. Many buyers will do a drive by and peek in your windows after hours. If they don't like what they see, they will call to reschedule the meeting, but what they are really doing is canceling the meeting. Make sure your windows are clean and have minimal signage. Too much signage and stickers in windows and doors are a huge distraction and not necessary.

Signage

This is crucial! You need good signage. Without proper signage, your buyers will not be able to find your location easily. Signage should be as big as your shopping center, landlord, and city ordinance will permit. It needs to be as large as possible and as visible as possible. If you are in an area with a lot of trees and shrubbery, then hire a gardener and clean it up. Have the gardener trim back the trees and shrubbery. Buyers and consumers need to see your sign not your pretty landscaping. Although pretty landscaping does help curb appeal, it cannot block your sign, door, sidewalk, or business. If you are in a strip mall then you need to have a sign on the strip mall's pylon so your buyers and consumers can locate your business. Your signage should not be antiquated and should be cleaned. I also recommend having a smaller sign on your door if you are in a strip mall. That way your customers and buyers can find your business easier.

Clean Interior

We talked about the outside; the outside sets the stage for what's on the inside. If the outside is dirty and cluttered, then buyers will walk in with an already negative perception of your business and will ultimately think the inside is dirty and cluttered.

Floors

Make sure the floors are clean. Painted concrete, hardwood floors, and tile all look good and are easy to clean and shine. Carpet is typically an issue. If the carpet is stained, you can have a professional shampoo it; however, I have seen a lot of stains come back. When carpet is stained or ripped, it gives the appearance that the business is dirty. There may be a lot of traffic, but if the owner is really making money like they say they are, then why don't they replace the carpet? Buyers will form their own perceptions on a multitude of things they see in your business. The less negativity we can create, the more positives we can show, and the more cash they will show at the closing table.

Walls

It's amazing how dirty walls and doors become and what a bad impression it leaves on buyers. Get some 409, put in some elbow grease, and get to work. It costs you almost nothing, but if you don't do it, it could cost you a lot.

Ceilings

Buyers will eyeball your entire space from the floors to the walls to the ceiling. I have seen a lot of businesses for sale and the business looks great until you look up and see the missing ceiling tiles. Go the extra mile and replace the ceiling tiles; again it is a cheap fix, but in the end will be worth it.

Clean It Up

There are a lot of manufacturing, construction, fabrication companies, and others that are not the most appealing businesses to show buyers.

Most of these businesses have a small office with a warehouse or plant attached to it with no AC, and a concrete floor, and with dirty, rusty equipment. Some of these buildings are covered in sheet metal and are certainly not attractive. My sellers always tell me, "It is what it is; we can't do anything to spruce it up." I disagree. You may not be able to stage it and make it look pretty, because let's face it, it is a shop. But, what you can do is clean it up. Power-wash the floor, and clean the bathrooms so it does not look like a bunch of hoodlums use it on a daily basis. Most importantly, clean the office. Create a nice space that the buyer can emotionally connect to and see themselves working there.

Again the industry will dictate how the business should look.

Stock Your Shelves

Retail locations should be stocked with inventory. There is nothing worse than bringing a buyer to see a grocery store, convenience store, or clothing store and the shelves/racks are empty. The buyers will automatically think that the seller has fallen on hard times and can't afford to stock the shelves. If your shelves are empty, then the buyer's pocketbook will be empty too, and they won't make you an offer. Stock your shelves.

No Dust

Shelves and inventory should be clean and free of dust. I showed a large all-in-one grocery store, deli, and gas station to a potential buyer. The shelves and inventory were covered in dust. It appeared as if no one had been shopping in the store for months. If so, then why are the products covered with dust? Get your employees to dust the shelves and inventory weekly. Needless to say, this buyer was not impressed and fussed about all the dust. I told my seller that I cannot and will not show his business anymore until they clean it up.

These are all easy, cost-effective solutions that will improve the look and feel of your business and leave your buyers with a good perception and wanting to see more.

To obtain a
"STAGE YOUR BUSINESS CHECKLIST," visit
www.betterbusinessbrokers.com
(877) 853-4227

CHAPTER TEN

The #1 Way to Ruin Your Business is to Tell People You're Selling Your Business

WHEN SELLING YOUR BUSINESS, CONFIDENTIALITY IS THE KEY TO MAINTAINING your business success. Confidentiality is the #1 reason sellers hire a business broker to handle the sale of their business. Telling people that you are selling your business is detrimental for a multitude of reasons, as we will discuss in this chapter.

People in general are very apprehensive and do not like change. One of the key ingredients in your business is your employees. Employees get spooked when they hear that the owner is selling the business. They automatically think that the new owner is going to come in and terminate them, cut their hours, or be difficult to work for. Employees start commiserating with each other and before you know it, you have a mess on your hands. In most cases, there is no reason to tell your employees that you are selling, unless you have a multimillion dollar company and the CFO needs to be privy to the sale in order to provide financials and facilitate the transaction. However, it is imperative to have the CFO or any other member of the management team sign

an NDA (non-disclosure agreement) before you engage their assistance.

The other key ingredient in your business is customers. Customers get spooked when they hear that the owner is selling the business. Customers do not like change either. They automatically think that the new owner is going to change things and not provide the same level of service. Customers have grown accustomed to the business's products, service, quality, and relationship with the owner and employees. This is not as big a problem in larger businesses where the owner is not as involved in the day-to-day operations and does not have a one-on-one relationship with the consumers. Customer's finding out the business is for sale can be detrimental in most cases. The best way to handle the sale of your business is not to tell the customers you're selling your business. In most situations, the owner and the buyer of the business do not tell customers until several months or years later that the business changed hands. Many sellers tell their customers that they took on a partner and the buyer does the same. This is especially helpful to say if you are owner financing part of your business.

> In most situations, the owner and the buyer of the business do not tell customers until several months or years later that the business changed hands.

Vendors are a key ingredient in your business as well. Without vendors, you have nothing to sell. Vendors also become concerned when they hear the business owner is selling the business. They automatically think that the new owner might have their own vendors or they will shop for new vendors. In many cases, vendors will have to financially qualify the new owner in order to purchase their products and services. In some scenarios the vendors will have to prequalify the buyer before the buyer can actually buy the business. This is especially true with distributors. Distributors have the right to determine if they are comfortable with the buyer's financials, skill sets, and industry experience.

Franchisors also get nervous that their franchisee is considering selling. They too will have to prequalify the buyer's financials, skill sets, and industry experience. Franchisors are typically not happy that the franchisee is selling because they have to train the new owner on running the business, their franchise formula, marketing, paperwork, and so much more. They have to support the new franchisee and get him/her up to speed. The new franchisee might not be as good as the previous one in running and marketing the business; therefore, the franchisor may end up losing money on royalties.

Landlords are an extremely important ingredient as well. If you are leasing space and your business is dependent on location loyalty, not brand loyalty, then you better hope your landlord will be cooperative with your buyer. Landlords are apprehensive and do not want to sign a new lease or transfer a lease to a new owner. They too do not know if the new owner will be successful, pay the rent on time, and take care of the property. They will also have to qualify the buyer's financials, skill sets, and industry experience before they agree to negotiate a new lease, transfer, or sublease. There is no reason to tell the landlord that you are selling until you have an offer with escrow money, unless you are on a month-to-month lease and cannot commit to a long-term lease for particular reasons. However, it is imperative to sign a one-year lease with renewal options if you have a month-to-month lease! If you stay on a month-to-month lease, then the buyer can and in most cases will go behind your back and negotiate directly with the landlord. This is especially true if the buyer is mostly interested in the location and not that interested in buying your business. Without a lease, you have nothing to sell.

Professionals get spooked as well. CPAs get nervous when an owner is selling because they think the buyer is going to have their own CPA and they will lose the business. In some cases this is true. Buyers will have their own CPA; however, you will in all likelihood have to discuss selling your business with your CPA at some point. You do not have to tell your CPA in the beginning of the process; however, it will be imperative to engage him/her during the due diligence process. Some buyers will want to conduct an audit of your books and records, at which point you will have to engage your CPA. Some buyers will hire a third-party forensic accountant to conduct the audit. The bottom line: Gather all your financial information from your accountant, and do not discuss the sale of the business until it becomes necessary. Your accountant is a professional and will still follow the code of ethics and handle your business in the utmost professional manner. It is not prudent to have your CPA do a valuation of your business. CPAs typically charge way too much to valuate a business, and in most cases their valuations are way off.

Attorneys are worried as well. They too believe the buyer will have their own attorney and they will also lose business. In many cases, attorneys overcharge and are deal killers when selling your business. They do not know how to valuate, sell, or prepare closing documents. It is imperative to utilize a business broker who has attorneys that are experienced in preparing closing documents or hire attorneys that are familiar with and experienced in business closings.

Competitors are not fearful that their competitor is selling their business. They are ecstatic that the owner is selling and will use it against them. They love to tell everyone they know, including their employees, vendors, and customers that their competitor is selling the business. In most cases they yell it from the roof tops: "ABC Company is going out of business!" This can be detrimental to your business as well.

Again, confidentiality is the number one reason sellers hire business brokers, not real estate agents, to sell their business. Your real estate agent's motto is: "The more people we tell, the more we sell." That motto will put you out of business very quickly!

Business brokers utilize their database of qualified buyers, advertise your businesses very confidentially, and only disclose your business to qualified buyers that have signed confidentiality agreements. In some cases, my firm does not disclose any proprietary details regarding the business until the seller is comfortable with the buyer's financials, skill sets, and industry experience. My firm facilitates this process by utilizing blind prospectuses and conference calls with the buyer and seller before any proprietary information is disclosed.

Confidentiality is usually never breached by the broker. It is typically breached by the owner telling acquaintances, clients, friends, and family that they are considering selling their business.

I listed a medical business for sale a few years ago. My seller was paranoid that his doctors would find out the business was for sale. Two months after signing the listing agreement, the seller called me in the middle of the night in a panic and wanted to know who I showed the business to. I told him that I had showed his business to one prospect. He was very upset and beside himself because all his doctors now knew he was thinking about selling his business. I then asked him, "Who did you tell?" He responded, "I did not tell anyone, other than my wife." I suggested to him that he try and calm down, get a good night's sleep, and think about whom else he discussed selling his business with. The next morning he called me and said, "I told a close friend that is a doctor that sends me business." Guess what? That doctor told a doctor that told a doctor that told another. Before you knew it, it spread like wildfire. Confidentiality is usually always breached by the seller, who tells someone who tells someone, etc., not the broker!

It is very difficult, almost impossible, to sell your business yourself without breaching confidentiality. Most sellers do not qualify buyers, nor do they get them to sign the proper non-disclosure documents.

> Business brokers utilize their database of qualified buyers, advertise your businesses very confidentially, and only disclose your business to qualified buyers that have signed confidentiality agreements.

Therefore, the buyer will tell their friends, family, and anyone else that they run into that they are considering buying that particular business.

In some situations it is imperative to have prospects sign not only an NDA, but a non-compete as well. There are sophisticated individuals out there that will pose as buyers, but all they are really interested in is finding out everything they can about a particular business or industry in order to compete with that business owner. I have heard horror stories where sellers gave potential buyers all kinds of proprietary information regarding their industry, systems, procedures, vendors, and customer lists. And at the end of the day, the buyer had everything they needed to compete against the seller. There is a fine line you walk in determining how much information you should share with a buyer during different phases of the buying process. My firm walks my sellers/buyers through every step of the process. We do not allow the seller to give away any proprietary information until we have an offer with escrow money on the table. We do not allow our sellers to give out their customer list or vendor list, or talk to employees until they actually go to close on the business.

Confidentiality is the most important step in the selling process, and if breached it will be detrimental to your business. It is crucial to maintain your business success and keep things running smoothly in order to sell your business without any bumps along the way.

For **NDA NON-DISCLOSURE AGREEMENT EXAMPLES,** visit www.betterbusinessbrokers.com (877) 853-4227

CHAPTER ELEVEN

Powerful Offering Memorandums That Will Leave the Buyer Wanting More

IT IS IMPERATIVE TO HAVE GOOD PAPER WHEN YOU PUT YOUR BUSINESS ON THE market. Buyers tell me constantly that they meet with business brokerage firms in order to gather information on a listing that they are interested in. It is amazing to me how many business brokers and real estate brokers do not put together a prospectus on the business. They give the buyers information that is scattered and piecemeal. The majority of sellers do not put together any prospectus or offering memorandum as well. Good, well-organized prospectuses will give the buyer plenty of information to determine if they want to move forward in seeing the business and negotiating a purchase offer on the business.

Many of my buyers will review the offering memorandum and decide if they want to move forward with the seller. My buyers will not waste my seller's time. If they are not truly interested, then they will not agree to take it to the next level and meet with the seller. The prospectus is designed to provide information, whet the buyer's appetite, and answer the majority of their questions. It is not designed to sell the business; it is designed to leave the buy-

ers wanting more. There are key elements that have to be included in the sale of the business, which we will discuss in greater detail below. The Offering Memorandum must include the following:

- **Ownership:** Who are the owners? All owners must be listed in the prospectus.

- **Entity:** What type of entity is this business? Is it an LLC, S Corp, C Corp, Partnership, or sole proprietorship?

- **Years in Business:** How long has the business been in existence and how long have you owned the business? As we discussed in previous chapters, the longer you have been in business, the greater the return when selling your business.

- **Location:** Where is the business located? How long have you been in that location? Does the owner own the real estate? Is the real estate for sale? Is there a lease? How much is the rent and what are the terms of the lease? Are there options to renew? Will the landlord allow for a transfer of the lease or agree to sublease? Is the business relocatable? What would it cost to move the business, if need be?

- **Business Summary:** Define what your business does and what makes your products and services unique.

- **Industry (strengths & weaknesses):** Describe your industry. What are the strengths and weaknesses of your particular industry?

- **Growth Potential:** What is the growth potential of your business and industry? How can someone grow your business? What would it take to catapult your business to the next level?

- **Competition:** Do you have competition? Who are they? What makes your products and services unique from your competitors? What can a buyer do to grow more market share?

- **Client Base:** Who are your customers? Do they do business with you due to brand loyalty, location loyalty, price, quality, customer service, or all of the above? What makes your customers buy from you? How far do your customers travel to purchase your products and services? Utilize graphs and charts to show your customer radius. What are the demographics of your clients; i.e., age, sex, and income range? You need to utilize charts and graphs to demonstrate your client's demographics as well. How much of your business is repeat business? Depending on your industry, you may have to list your customers by number (not name) and list them from top to bottom as it relates to the amount of money they spend monthly with your business. You can also pull a customer report from QuickBooks or any other software program you utilize. You can easily remove the customer names from this report. What percentage of your revenue comes from what percentage of your clients? Does your business follow the 80/20 rule? Or do you have one or two customers that make up the majority of your revenue? I have an office supply company listed. Our offering memorandum utilizes charts and graphs to show their client mix. For example: 65 percent of their business is government contracts, 25 percent is commercial clients, and the rest are schools.

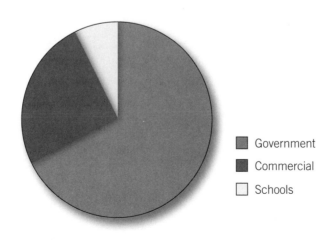

How do you obtain new clients? How much does it cost you to acquire a new client?

- **Contracts in Place:** Do you have any contracts in place? How many? What are the length and terms of the contracts? Are your contracts transferable? If your contracts are not transferable, then it could cause issues with the new owner. The buyer may have to purchase your business as a stock sale in order to ensure they are able to retain those customers.
- **Product Mix:** Describe your product mix by utilizing graphs and charts. Do you have additional revenue streams? If so, utilize a graph showing what percentage of the business comes from which profit center? Example: I have an AC & Manufacturing company. Fifty percent of their business is AC & Heating and the other fifty percent is manufacturing.

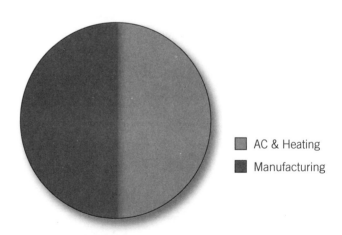

You need to let the buyer know if the companies can be split up and sold to different buyers. An AC & Heating technician might love to purchase the AC & Heating division, but has absolutely no interest in the manufacturing business. However, there are a lot of manufacturing companies that would be interested in the manufacturing business, but not the AC & Heating business.

- **Logos, Trademarks, or Trade Secrets:** Identify your logo and trademarks. Make it clear in the prospectus that you have trade secrets, but do not disclose all your trade secrets on paper before you close on the business. For instance, if you own a restaurant, you don't give away your recipes until the buyer has purchased the business. I have a food manufacturing company listed. They have eight trademarks and a hundred and fifty different trademarked secret recipes. We are disclosing the trademarks in the prospectus, but not the recipes. If someone wants the recipes, then they have to buy the business.

- **Seasonality:** Is your business seasonal? If so, when and how long is your season? What types of revenue do you generate in the busy season compared to the slow season? How much working capital is needed during the slow season? Are there any other profit centers or revenue streams that you can introduce in the slow season to generate more revenue during the slow months? My AC & Heating company mentioned above did just that. Their AC business is very busy during the summer months and tends to dramatically slow down in the winter. Therefore, they started the manufacturing business that generates a steady flow of revenue all year round. This additional profit center assists them in getting through the slow season and provides for a healthy cash flow year round.

- **Advertising:** Explain your advertising methods. Do you advertise? What methods of advertising do you utilize? What is your advertising budget? Do you get co-op money for advertising? If so, how much? I have a motorcycle dealership for sale. They carry three different franchises. Each franchise provides advertising dollars annually, depending upon certain criteria that the dealership must follow. If you were going to grow the business, which advertising methods and/ or vehicle would you use?

- **Internet Presence:** Do you have a Website? Is it up to date? Who hosts your site? Do you sell products online? Do you engage in social networking? Who keeps up with that in your business? Can you grow your business via the internet and social media?

- **Employees and Management Team:** Describe your management team and employees by utilizing an organizational chart. Define who your employees are, their tenure with the company, their job title, and their pay. The larger the company, the more detailed you need to be. Do you have employee contracts? Do you have any non-compete agreements? Do you have any independent contractors that work for you, and how are they paid? Do you offer employee benefits? What are they? What is your employee retention rate? Do you have a human resource manager on staff? How much does it cost you to hire and train new staff? Larger companies need to identify their key personnel, such as CEO, CFO, Operations Manager, and any other key employees. Do the employees know the business is for sale? Do you think the employees will stay on for the new owner? What key employees, if any, will assist with the sale of the business?

- **Business Strengths:** Be sure to identify all your business strengths and what makes your business unique. Utilize bullets to list your strengths so they clearly stand out.

- **Business Weaknesses:** Identify your business weaknesses as opportunities for growth. Give the buyer some ideas of how they can grow the business and make it even better. This too should be done by utilizing bullets to outline opportunities for growth.

- **Training After the Sale:** You need to identify how long you are willing to train the new owner. The length of training will vary greatly depending upon the industry, special skills needed, and the buyer's experience level and skill sets. Small businesses, such as coffee shops, conveniences stores, etc., will train for 2-3 days. Restaurants, bars, clothing stores, day cares, etc., will train for 2-3 weeks. Larger companies will need to train for 1-4 months. Training is included in the price of the business. Buyers should not have to pay extra for training. There is a big difference between training and working. You are there to train the new owner, not to work for them. I personally explain that to all my buyers. Some companies will require that the owner stay on for an extended period of time, for which the owner will be compensated. Some owners might also stay on as a consultant to the new owner as well. You need to identify if you are willing to stay on for the new owner and in what capacity and at what cost.

- **Franchise Information (if applicable):** If your business is a franchise, then it is important that you include information regarding the franchise in your prospectus. My firm includes information regarding franchise corporate headquarters, franchisee qualifications, application process, training, transfer fee, and closing protocol.

- **After the Sale:** You need to agree and outline in the prospectus the non-compete that you will agree to. Noncompete laws are different from state to state. Seek advice from a business broker or an attorney regarding what is enforceable in your particular state. In Louisiana, the noncompete law is for 2 years and has to be identified by a specific parish or parishes. Buyers will need a non-compete to provide them with peace of mind that you are not going to sell your business, cash out, and then go down the street and compete against them.

- **FF&E List:** Make sure that you have an Excel spreadsheet that outlines your furniture, fixtures, and equipment that will be included in the sale. This list will become your bible and will be part of the closing documents. You need to identify everything that is included and document the items. Make sure you include the manufacturer (if applicable), serial number (if applicable), VIN number (if you have vehicles or heavy equipment), year and make of vehicles included. Make sure you include quantities of tables, chairs, etc. It is imperative that you also list things that are not included. If you have a Mercedes that you pay for through the business, but which you are not including in the sale of the business, then you must record this car on the NOT IN-CLUDED list. It is very important to have an "included list" and a "not included list." I was sitting at the closing table for a multimillion dollar business. When the attorneys started going through the closing documents, they started discussing the FF&E list included in the sale. The buyer mentioned that the large flat screen television located in the seller's conference room was not on the list and needed to be added. The seller said in response, "The TV is not included and I am taking it home." The buyer was furious; he started yelling, "This is ridiculous after all the money I am spending on this business, the TV had better be included or I am not purchasing your business." The seller's attorney said that the TV is listed on the not included list; therefore it is not included. All parties reviewed the not included list and the flat screen TV was not listed! The buyer and seller started yelling at each other. So, of course, I thought it was ridiculous on the part of both parties. The seller was making a fortune on the sale of his business, so he could have easily included the TV. The buyer was spending millions on the business; therefore, spending another thousand is not really much considering the big picture. Neither side was budging, so I jumped up and yelled, "Everyone calm down; I will buy another flat screen TV for the conference room." So I went to Best Buy that day and purchased the TV; therefore, everyone was happy and the deal closed. The moral of the story is to make sure if you are not including it then record it on the "not included list." In addition, it is imperative that you keep up with your included and not included lists. Sellers are notorious for replacing, removing, and adding equipment. If you removed something and did not replace it, then you will probably have to replace that piece of equipment before selling the business. The buyer has every right to walk through your business before the close with the FF&E checklist and mark what is there, what is missing, and what is not working. The seller has to honor the FF&E list and make sure that everything is there and is in working condition. Please make sure you notify your broker when removing, replacing, or adding FF&E. We do not want any surprises at the closing table, nor do you want to pay out of pocket to replace the FF&E that you removed. My firm constantly updates our FF&E list for our sellers. However, we won't know if something has changed unless we are notified by the seller.

- **Financials:** It is imperative to include a three to five year financial spreadsheet based on your tax returns and profit and loss statements. You must identify your add backs in the spreadsheet in order to show the buyer what your true seller's discretionary income, EBITDA or EBIT, is. This financial spreadsheet will aid in supporting your asking price. Do not include your tax returns or P&L in the prospectus. They are not necessary. You should not give your tax returns or other financial statements to any buyers without having an offer on the table with escrow money. You can show your statements in your office to a buyer, but don't let them walk out the door with your financials. The financial spreadsheet will provide buyers with enough information in order to move forward.

- **Price & Terms:** The last page of your prospectus should include a Price & Terms Sheet. This sheet should outline the price of the FF&E, inventory, cash flow, real estate (if applicable), AR, working capital (if applicable), and any other intellectual property. It should also state any transfer fees (if your business is a franchise). Everything should be added up to show how you came up with the total price of your business. Inventory should always be included in the sale of the business. The buyer/seller will take inventory the day before closing or they will agree on a third-party inventory company to do so. Inventory will be adjusted upward or downward at closing. AR (accounts receivables) is usually included in the sale of the business; however, it sometimes becomes a negotiating tool. Working capital is often included in larger companies only. Again, it too is a negotiating tool. If you are a franchise, then a transfer fee has to be paid and the buyer usually pays that as well. However, it too is a negotiating tool and sometimes the seller will agree to pay the transfer fee.

Make sure you include color photos, graphs, and charts in your prospectus. Most individuals are visual and pictures are worth a thousand words. You can sell your business much better by including photos of the outside and inside of your business. Also, be sure to include menus, spa service menus, and any other brochures or marketing pieces that describe your products and services.

Your offering memorandum should be reviewed only by qualified buyers who have signed an NDA and have provided their financial statement. Your offering memorandum is the first step in getting buyers interested in your business. If you are going to engage a business brokerage firm to handle the sale of your business, then make sure you ask to see some examples of completed prospectuses they have produced.

For **EXAMPLES OF PROSPECTUSES,** visit
www.betterbusinessbrokers.com
(877) 853-4227

CHAPTER TWELVE

Marketing Your Business for Sale Without Breaching Confidentiality

MARKETING YOUR BUSINESS FOR SALE WITHOUT BREACHING CONFIDENTIALITY IS almost impossible to do on your own. This process is difficult for a variety of reasons. Below are the questions you need to ask yourself before putting your business up for sale.

- What description are you going to use on the internet without breaching confidentiality?
- What email address are you going to use in the ads?
- What phone number are you going to provide in the ads?
- What fax number are you going to provide to potential prospects to fax?
- What NDAs (non-disclosures agreements) are you going to utilize?
- Where are you going to meet prospects?
- How are you going to determine who is on the other end of the phone or email address when communicating with them? How do you know who you are really talking to? It could be your acquaintance, vendors, customers, or employees making contact with you.

These individuals too look at businesses to purchase. In addition, competitors are always looking to obtain information on their competition; therefore, if they see an ad for their competitor they may act like an interested buyer in order to obtain information.

The above questions will help you determine if you think you can sell your business on your own without breaching confidentiality.

Below are some tips to help you market your business as discreetly as possible and tips to help you eliminate the most common mistakes sellers make when marketing their business for sale.

Hire a professional, experienced business broker

Again, this is the number one reason sellers hire business brokers. Business brokers are very successful at marketing businesses without breaching confidentiality.

Do not hire a real estate agent

As mentioned in previous chapters, real estate agents' motto is "the more people I tell, the more I sell." They do not utilize ten to twenty business MLS (multiple listing sites) to advertise businesses. They typically place the business owner's ad on the MLS (real estate listing site), not business sites. The real estate MLS site is not the most productive site to market businesses, and in most cases it is not the most confidential site because you have to include proprietary information such as the business address. The real estate multiple listing site is typically just used for real estate, not businesses that are trying to maintain confidentiality. In addition, real estate agents will put a sign in the front yard or window (if permitted) and occasionally run an ad in the paper.

Don't place signs up in or around your business

It is a huge mistake to put for sale signs up in your business. It shows desperation on the owner's behalf and causes a bad perception for employees, vendors, and customers.

Advertise discretely on business internet sites

There are anywhere between ten to twenty business MLS sites that you can discretely market your business on. You should place you business on all of them, if possible. It is imperative to maximize visibility in order to attract as many buyers as possible. You will have to pay a monthly fee for each one of these sites. You will also have to post your listing to all these sites, which can take hours to accomplish. You will also have to update these sites on a regular basis so they appear at the top of the list. Please keep in mind that most business brokers will pay for the MLS fees and post and update your listing to all these different sites regularly, which will save you a tremendous amount of time, money, energy, and effort. If you are attempting to sell your business on your own, then keep in mind that you will have to screen all buyers from these sites to determine which buyers are a good fit for your business. Again, this takes an enormous amount of time and energy and can lead to breaching confidentiality if handled by the seller. Many buyers are tire kickers and are not qualified to buy your business. In my firm, we kiss a lot of frogs before we find our prince of a buyer to purchase a business. In addition, ninety five percent of buyers do not buy the business they called in on. Therefore, that only gives you a five percent chance to sell your business. Business brokers will have a lot more buyers, because they have a lot more inventory than one business that the buyer ninety five percent of the time will not buy.

Advertise in newspapers and trade journals

You can advertise in newspapers and trade journals very discretely. However, again you have to determine what contact information you are going to include in the ad. Also, keep in mind that advertising is very expensive and you have to advertise consistently in order to attract the right buyer.

These are all good tips that provide the do's and don'ts that a seller can utilize; however, you still run a risk when attempting to market your business for sale on your own. The one thing you do not want to do when marketing your business for sale is to tell anyone that you are selling your business. This is a sure fire way to breach confidentiality and put your business at risk.

Most, not all, business brokers will utilize the above mentioned marketing strategies. My firm implements a very strategic and comprehensive marketing plan for each one of our individual businesses. I am not going to disclose all of our marketing techniques in this book; however, we do have a database of thousands of buyers for all types of businesses. In addition, we have a database of private equity firms and strategic buyers. We also subscribe to a multitude of lists in order to implement strategic marketing campaigns.

To see if **WE HAVE BUYERS FOR YOUR BUSINESS,** visit www.betterbusinessbrokers.com
(877) 853-4227

CHAPTER THIRTEEN

Interviewing, Educating, and Qualifying Buyers Before They Kick the Tires

WORKING WITH BUYERS IS A HUGE UNDERTAKING. YOU CANNOT JUST SHOW A buyer your business and then expect them to maintain confidentiality, negotiate a purchase offer, and give you money. You have to interview them first to see if they are a good fit for your business before disclosing any proprietary information. Then you have to qualify the buyer to make sure they can operate your business. You also have to financially qualify the buyer to make sure they can afford to purchase your business. In addition, you have to educate the buyer. If you do not properly educate the buyer and plan for buyer's remorse, then I can assure you that your deal will fall apart and you just wasted all your time, energy, and effort. We will discuss interviewing, educating, and qualifying buyers in great detail in this chapter.

As we discussed in the previous chapter, ninety five percent of buyers do not buy the business they called about; therefore, you need to do the following:

Interview Buyers

Find out what their previous experience has been in. What are their skill sets? What are their dreams and desires? What are their hot buttons? Why do they want to own a business or purchase another business? Who is going to run the business? Most importantly, what is their WHY? Why do they want to buy your business; why do they want to own their own business? If you do not uncover their why, then you will not be able to sell them your business.

To obtain the **"BUYER'S INTERVIEW WORKSHEET,** visit www.betterbusinessbrokers.com
(877) 853-4227

Qualify Buyers On:

Financial capability

You must obtain a financial statement. You have to evaluate how much cash they have in their checking and savings account. How much do they have in their retirement fund, equity in their home, and any other sources of assets they can borrow against? How much are they earning now? Will they continue to keep their current business and/or job? Will their current income continue? You have to review their liabilities in order to determine their net worth. If a buyer does not have any cash, that does not mean they cannot buy your business. As mentioned above, how much do they have in retirement? Buyers can borrow against their retirement fund to purchase a business without paying taxes and penalties. However, you will need to know who to put the buyer in contact with so they can set up their C Corporation in order to accomplish this. Many CPAs—not all— are not aware of this process and cannot assist their clients with this type of transaction. If the buyer has a little cash but no retirement, they may have equity in their home that they can get a line of credit against. However, getting a home equity loan or line of credit is not as easy as it once was due to the financial debacle and today's economy. If the buyer has any cash, retirement, equity, or another business they can borrow against, then there is a possibility that the buyer is qualified and you may just have to get creative on how you structure the deal. You also have to make sure that you tell the buyer that the only way they can afford to purchase your business is if they use their cash, borrow against their retirement, or get a home equity loan. Some buyers will jump through those hoops, and other buyers will not. This is when you obtain a commitment that they are willing to take those steps, perhaps even before you hand over all your proprietary information on your business. If they are not willing to move forward, then they are not serious. Buyers need to start the ball rolling on their retirement fund, home equity loan, and/or cash, or any other type of loan before they make a decision on what business they are going to buy. Just because a buyer obtains the money via their retirement or home equity does not mean they have to use it. However, the good thing is that they will have all their funds and ducks in a row when they are ready to pull the trigger. If the buyer does not have enough cash for a solid down payment or money in their retirement fund or equity in their house and they tell you that they can acquire the money from a family member, partner, or investor, in all likelihood that is not going to happen. These deals typically never ever come to fruition! If buyers cannot demonstrate that they have or can get the funds, then I strongly suggest that you walk away from those buyers. My firm does not waste our time, or more importantly our seller's time, on buyers that cannot qualify to purchase the business. In all my years of experience in selling businesses and dealing with buyers, I can count on one hand how many times these types of buyer were actually able to obtain the funds to purchase the business. My firm insists that the buyer bring the investor to the table and that investor must provide financial statements, sign an NDA, and convince me that they are willing to invest their money. Otherwise we walk away and so should you! In addition, if there is going to be a seller financing component to the transaction, then you may need to pull credit and/or have the buyer print out their most recent credit report for your review.

Skill set

Depending upon your industry you really need to qualify the buyer to see if they have the required skills, experience, licenses, and wherewithal to run your business. If they don't have the skills and or licenses and they do not have anyone in mind to run the business, then they are probably not a good fit for your business.

Time frame

This is a very important qualifier as well. You have to know the buyer's time frame. I had a buyer meeting the other day, and I asked the buyer what his time frame was. He replied, "A year." "A year?" I said. "Why did you call me to look at the business?" I told him, "It is way too premature for you to look at anything for a multitude of reasons. If I show you a business and you like it, it probably will not still be on the market in a year. More importantly, I am not going to waste my seller's time meeting with you if you cannot purchase anything for a year." This particular buyer was adamant regarding the year time frame because he had been employed for years with the same company and was waiting on his retirement package. He did not want to purchase a business until he retired in a year. He was not willing to allow anyone else to manage the company for him during that year while he continued to work in his job. He was meticulous and picky and wanted to be a hands-on owner. Therefore, I educated him on the buying process and told him to come see me within three months prior to purchasing a business. Timing is everything and if the buyer is not ready to purchase in the next few months, then you should not waste your time and energy with that particular buyer.

Decision making

Who else is involved in the decision making process? If you are meeting with the husband or wife in regards to purchasing your business, you had better meet with the spouse as well. Spouses kill deals too if they are not part of the process and are not on board. If the buyer needs or has a partner or needs investors, then you need to qualify that person or individuals as well. Make sure that all parties involved sign an NDA and provide a financial statement.

Educate Buyers on the Buying Process

Confidentiality

You have to stress the importance of confidentiality to your buyers. If you don't, they will not take you seriously and will disclose your proprietary information to their friends, family, and associates. My firm puts the fear of God into our buyers. We tell them that if they breach confidentiality, then the seller will file suit and we will have no other choice than to join the seller in the lawsuit. We explain to the buyers that breaching confidentiality can and will ruin the seller's business, and we do not want to ruin the business before they buy the business.

Touring the business

You need to educate the buyers on the process of seeing the business. If it is a retail location, then you can tell the buyer that they can come by at any time and act as a customer and purchase products and services. However, make sure you enforce the fact that they are not allowed to talk to any of the employees; nor are they allowed to walk in with the prospectus or any other marketing materials on the business. You should educate them that you will show them the business after hours only; therefore, no employees are privy to the conversations.

When to conduct due diligence

You need to educate your buyers on what and how much due diligence you are going to allow them to do before they make an offer. That will be your determination. However, buyers are not going to make offers without seeing financials, seeing the business, and getting the majority of their questions answered. Besides, you should want the buyer to make an offer based on education, not pressure. A lot of brokers/sellers pressure buyers into making offers just to gather information. There are many issues associated with that theory. First and foremost, how does a buyer know what to offer if he or she has not seen any financials? An offer based on education is far better than an offer based on pressure. In my firm, the majority of the buyer's due diligence is done upfront. Therefore, when the buyer makes the offer, the buyer is comfortable with their decision and is making an educated offer. That is the main reason why I close 98% of all offers I write. My competitors close less than 40% of offers they write. Less than 40% of all transactions handled between a buyer/seller actually close. The majority of them fall apart because the buyer was never qualified in the first place. Tell your qualified buyers that you will allow them to do the majority of their due diligence upfront, such as reviewing the offering memorandum, financials, seeing the business, and getting the majority of their questions answered. However, you are not going to allow other forms of due diligence until you have an offer with escrow money on the table.

Some examples of due diligence are:

- Conducting an audit of the books and records
- Meeting with the landlord to negotiate a lease

- Obtaining franchise approval (if applicable)
- Obtaining a commercial loan or an SBA loan

These are all example of due diligence items that should require an offer accompanied by escrow. You do not want to jump through hoops to help a buyer negotiate a lease or get financing if you have not even had a meeting of the minds as it relates to price and terms. Therefore, you must have an offer with escrow.

To obtain an **EXAMPLE OF A BUYER'S FINANCIAL FORM,** visit
www.betterbusinessbrokers.com
(877) 853-4227

Educate Buyers on Business Valuations

Some buyers are educated and understand how valuations are done. Most buyers are not educated and have no idea. You should educate your buyer on how you arrived at your asking price. The more the buyer knows and understands the valuation, the more they will be willing to pay for your business. Every industry is different and has different formulas. Most businesses are calculated on the classifications listed below.

- **Gross:** Some businesses are calculated on a percentage of your gross income plus/or including the inventory.

- **EBITDA:** A lot of businesses are calculated on Earnings before interest, taxes, depreciation, and amortization plus/or including inventory.

- **EBIT:** Some businesses are calculated on a multiple Earnings before interest and taxes plus/or including inventory.

- **SDE:** Some businesses are calculated on a multiple of the seller's true discretionary earnings plus/or including inventory. This would include all the seller's add back of personal expenses they run through their business and non-recurring expenses.

- **Net Income:** Some businesses are calculated on a multiple of the net income that is reflected on the tax returns plus/or including the inventory, plus/or including the FF&E.

- **Years in Business:** You need to educate the buyer that the longer a business has been in business, then the greater the multiple that business has earned.

- **Intellectual property:** The multiple is also determined by how much intellectual property is included in the business such as trademarks and trade secrets.

- **Location:** Location, location, location will cause some businesses to sell for more than others if they have a dynamite location with real estate or a solid lease in place.

- **FF&E:** You need to explain to the buyers that there is real value to the FF&E in most cases and this number is added or included in the sales price of the business. However, please keep in mind that FF&E depreciates significantly and is not worth what you think it is worth. In most cases FF&E is included in the multiple. If not, then you should have an appraisal on your FF&E or a used price list on all your furniture, fixtures, and equipment.

- **Inventory:** You have to educate the seller on the fact that the inventory is included in the sale of the business at cost and will be adjusted upward or downward depending on the inventory count at close.

- **AR (accounts receivables):** You need to explain how AR works and it too will be included in the sales price. However, it may not be included if the buyer is negotiating to pay less than the asking price of the business. AR is only viable to buyers if you can demonstrate a ninety percent collection rate or better on an aging report's one to three years' history. Buyers are not interested in becoming a collection agency in order to get paid at the end of the day.

- **AP (accounts payables):** You have to educate buyers on accounts payables. Accounts payable is usually paid by the seller, though not always. It depends on whether the business is a stock sale or an asset sale. It also depends on who is getting paid for the work that has been completed or the work in progress and what payables are associated with those particular jobs. This has to be determined before you write a purchase offer.

- **Working Capital:** You have to educate the buyer on how much working capital is needed in your business and when they may need more to carry them through the slow seasons. In addition, you need to let the buyer know if the working capital is included in the company's bank account. Some sellers include the working capital and some do not. As discussed in the previous chapters, you need to make that determination before you price the business for sale.

- **Transfer Fee (if applicable):** If you are a franchise then you need to educate the buyer on the transfer fee that will have to be paid. You also need to educate the buyer on the franchisor's qualifications, training, and requirements. You typically cannot close on a franchise until the franchisee has been approved, the FDD (franchise disclosure document) must be signed, and the training must be completed. Some franchisors take 3 to 6 months to close. The offer must be contingent on franchise approval.

Educate Buyers on Financing

Commercial Lending

If the buyer thinks they are going to get commercial financing, then they are probably not educated and are in serious need of a reality check, especially in today's economy and given our financial debacle. Banks will lend if the perfect storm occurs. The perfect storm means that the seller must have great books and records with very little add backs. The cash flow of the business must support the debt service and leave the buyer enough income to live on. The buyer must have perfect credit, cash on hand for a twenty five to thirty percent down payment, enough collateral to secure the loan, and industry experience. I can tell you in all of my years of experience, the perfect storm rarely occurs. Lenders are also very particular on what they will lend on. They do not like restaurants, bars, and many other industries.

SBA Lending

It is not nearly as easy to get an SBA loan as it once was. SBA is also very selective as to what they will and will not lend on. They too want perfect books and records. They too want the buyer to have perfect credit, collateral to secure the loan, and twenty to thirty percent down. They want the seller to share the risk as well and hold paper subordinate to their loan. They too want the buyer to have industry experience. They are usually two points above prime and do not fix the interest rate. Therefore, the buyer will have a variable rate that can and will fluctuate. The increase in interest will have a negative effect on what the new owner will profit from the business. SBA can take as long as six months to close and is very paperwork intensive. Most sellers do not want to go through the process and take their business off the market for something that may or may not happen.

Seller's Financing

This is something that you as a seller need to understand and be open-minded to. As mentioned before, banks are not doing loans unless the perfect storm has occurred. Therefore, if you want to sell your business, then you must be creative. In my firm, a hundred percent of my sellers have agreed to some seller financing upfront. Buyers know that sellers are holding paper and almost all sellers have become the bank. If you are going to seller finance, then you need to educate the buyer on what forms of security and language need to be in place in order for you to help guarantee that you will get paid at the end of the day. Please refer to the bonus section of this book to gain insight on how to secure and ensure that you will get paid on your business.

Home Equity Loan

If a buyer is going to get a home equity loan, then the banks will take several things into consideration. Banks will look at the ability to repay the loan. Can the buyer pay it from their current income and are they keeping their job? Most financial institutions want to know why the buyer is obtaining a home equity loan. If the buyer is using the funds to buy a business, then the bank might request the business financials, a prospectus, a business plan, and the buyer's resume. The bank will have an appraiser do a drive by to see if the home appraises for the amount the buyer wants to borrow. Obtaining a home equity loan is not a slam dunk in today's economy.

Borrowing Against Retirement Fund

This is how deals are getting done these days. The buyer borrows from their retirement fund without paying taxes and penalties in order to obtain a forty to sixty percent deposit. The seller holds the note on the remaining balance. You need to be able to direct the buyer to the proper resources and specialists in order to facilitate this process.

Educate Buyers on the Seller's Sanity Check

You need to educate buyers on what sellers look at when selling their business. Most sellers are concerned in regards to who buys their business. They want to make sure that the new owner will take care of their employees and customers. They want to make sure that they are leaving their baby in good hands. The seller needs to educate the buyer on negotiations. The buyer cannot have their cake and eat it too. They cannot negotiate heavily on the asking price and then ask the seller to share the risk and provide seller financing. You need to educate the buyer on the fact that the seller needs to be compensated fairly for their years in business, location, proprietary systems, trademarks, proven systems, customer base, employees in place, and all the time, energy, and effort they have put into the business.

Educate Buyers on Making an Offer

- **Asset versus Stock Sale:** Sellers and buyers need to understand the difference between an asset and a stock sale. Ninety-nine percent of all transactions are asset sales. Buyers prefer asset sales because they can depreciate the assets and they are not liable for any liabilities or outstanding taxes that took place on the seller's watch. Buyers do not want to be liable for any lawsuits, liabilities, or unpaid taxes. Sellers prefer stock sales because it decreases their tax liability. However, there are different ways for sellers to decrease their tax liability. Stock sales become necessary if the business has contracts or licenses that are in the company name and cannot be transferred to another entity.

- **Asset Sale:** If the business is an asset sale, then the buyer must form a new corporation. If the buyer is borrowing money from their retirement fund, then they will need to set up a C Corp. If not, the buyer can set up an LLC, S Corp, or any other entity they prefer. The new entity will be doing business as the existing company's name.

- **EIN Number:** Educate the buyer that they will need to acquire a new tax ID number before closing on the business.

- **Escrow:** You need to tell the buyers that they will have to put up escrow money when purchasing your business. The standard amount in the industry is ten percent of the purchase price.

- **Contingencies:** Explain to the buyer that you will write contingencies into the purchase offer, such as negotiating the lease, obtaining franchise approval, obtaining financing, etc. These contingencies are there to allow the buyer to conduct their due diligence and protect their escrow funds. If the buyer cannot obtain the lease, franchise approval, or any other contingency, then there is no deal and the buyer is entitled to receive their escrow deposit back in two to three business days.

The Closing Process

- **Completing due diligence:** You need to explain to the buyer that there will be a due diligence period and a due diligence expiration date in which to complete and address their contingencies.

- **Closing attorney and closing documents:** You need to educate the buyer on the closing process and choosing a closing attorney. It is the attorney's job to make sure that there are no outstanding liabilities and or tax issues. It is also the attorney's job to construct legal documents based upon the purchase offer. It is not the attorney's job to renegotiate the deal. The price and terms have already been agreed upon by seller and buyer. This is where things tend to get tricky. If the buyer and seller both hire their own attorney, then the two attorneys usually end up trying to renegotiate the deal and raise obstacles and create issues that did not exist. Most attorneys bill per hour; the more issues they cause, the more they increase their bill. I represented a two million dollar medical company where my firm recommended an attorney that was going to facilitate the close and not represent either party, but represent the transaction and charge $5,000 for the closing. The buyer was very insistent on using a family friend. I asked the buyer if the attorney had any experience in representing and preparing closing documents for business closings. He replied, "He did not; however, he worked for a very large corporate firm." The seller hired his own attorney. The buyer's attorney ended up going two weeks past the closing date. He constantly tried to renegotiate the deal. He was extremely unprofessional; he yelled and screamed and cussed everyone out. In fact, the attorney went so far as to say he did not want to do the deal. Of course, that is where I had to step in and tell the attorney to back off! This is not his deal to do! I then pulled both buyer/seller into a separate conference room and proceeded to ask the buyer and seller if they wanted to continue with the transaction. They both said yes, but were extremely frustrated that the attorney was renegotiating everything that they had already agreed to. I then told the buyer that he needed to control his attorney. The attorney works for him, not the other way around. I told them if we continue down this path, then nothing is going to get solved, and the buyer and seller will begin to have animosity towards each other. The buyer then decided to grow a pair and control his attorney. Needless to say, the deal did get done, but not without a very expensive price tag! Remember, I had an attorney that agreed to a flat fee of $5,000 to facilitate the entire transaction? The buyer's attorney charged him a whopping $35,000 and the seller's attorney charged him a whopping $30,000. If they would have taken my advice and listened to me—"the professional"—they would have saved an astonishing $60,000.

The moral of this story: Hire a business broker who hires the attorneys or locates an attorney with experience closing business deals, agree to a flat fee for the transaction, and have the buyer split the attorney's fee with you. Attorneys kill deals. You must hire an attorney on a flat fee that represents the transaction, not their bank account. Both buyer and seller should always have their individual attorney review the closing documents.

- **Taking Inventory:** As mentioned in previous chapters, educate the buyer on inventory. Inventory is calculated at cost and is included in the purchase price of the business. Inventory will be taken by buyer/seller or a third-party inventory company that both parties agree to. Buyer and seller will split the cost. Inventory will be adjusted upward or downward at closing depending upon the inventory count.
- **FF&E Inspection:** Educate the buyer that they will be able to do a walk through to make sure that all the FF&E on the list is there and in good working condition.
- **Seller Training:** Let the buyer know what skills are necessary to run your business and inform the buyer of how long you are willing to train without pay. Also let the buyer know if you are willing to stay on as an employee or consultant. Make sure you discuss pay and terms if staying on in any capacity.
- **Non-Compete:** You will give the buyer tremendous peace of mind by telling them that you will sign a non-compete and you have no desire in going back into that particular industry.

Transfer

- **Lease:** It is very important to tell the buyer that he/she is not allowed to contact the landlord whatsoever till there is an agreed upon offer with escrows. A new lease, a transfer, or a sublease needs to be in place and signed by the landlord and buyer before or on the closing day.
- **Utilities:** Tell the buyer that they will have to transfer all utilities and phones. The transfer date will take place on the day of closing. The buyer may have to put down new deposits and the seller should receive their initial deposits back.
- **Insurance:** Insurance is not typically transferable. Therefore, the buyer needs to obtain insurance before the closing.

- **Taxes:** Taxes will be paid by the seller up to the day of closing. Any taxes incurred after the day of closing are the buyer's responsibility.

- **Bank Accounts:** Educate the buyer that they will have to set up their own bank account. However, they cannot do this until they have set up their new entity, DBA, and EIN number.

- **Credit Card Machine:** If your business takes credit cards, then you need to work with the buyer to transfer the credit card machine over to the buyer's account on the day of closing. You have to contact the credit card company in advanced so the transfer takes place on the closing date. If this cannot be done then the attorney needs to insert language in the closing documents stating that all money coming in from credit card transactions on the day of closing or the day after closing will be transferred to the buyer's account immediately.

To obtain the **"BUYER'S TRANSFER CHECKLIST,"** visit www.betterbusinessbrokers.com
(877) 853-4227

When to Discuss the Sale With Employees

Educate your buyer that they are not to talk to your employees whatsoever until you give written permission to do so. When to talk to employees really depends on what type and size of company you are selling. Small businesses do not tell the employees till after the closing. Larger companies will typically have one to two key employees involved in the transaction. Upon closing, the seller will communicate the sale of the business to the rest of their team after the closing. Some sellers/buyers will agree to have a sit down meeting with the owner's staff after the due diligence expiration date and the deposit is now non-refundable.

When to Discuss the Sale with Customers

Most sellers do not tell any customers until the business closing is completed. A lot of sellers/buyers will agree not to tell customers that the business has been sold for months to years after the transaction. Sellers feel more comfortable that the buyer does not broadcast the sale of the business if there is a seller financing component. Many buyers would prefer to say that they have partnered with the seller or they give themselves some new title such as CFO, CEO, or Regional Manager. No matter which way you and the buyer decide to handle it, it is imperative that you introduce the buyer to as many customers as you possibly can in order to ensure a smooth transition.

Vendors

Tell your buyer that you will introduce them to all vendors after the sale of the business.

Franchisor

You will obviously have to tell the franchisor before marketing your business for sale or as soon as you receive a purchase offer with escrow. Upon receiving a purchase offer, the franchisor can begin the qualification process. If the franchisor does not approve the buyer, then you have the right to know the reason for denial and you will need to search for another buyer. My firm takes back up offers on all businesses. We never put our eggs in one buyer's basket because the deal can fall apart at any one of these above obstacles we have been discussing.

Again, education is the key to success in selling your business. If you do not properly interview and educate the buyer on all the above mentioned items, then your buyer will not be prepared, perhaps not be serious, and your deal will fall apart.

CHAPTER FOURTEEN

Tips on Getting the Buyer to Emotionally Connect to Your Business

PEOPLE BUY BASED ON EMOTIONS, NOT NECESSARILY LOGIC. HOWEVER, WHEN buying a business the logic has to be there. The numbers have to make sense and meet the buyer's sanity check; otherwise, the buyer will not continue the buying process on your particular business. Therefore, if the numbers make sense, then you need to connect the buyer emotionally to your business. If the buyer does not have a warm and fuzzy feeling and an emotional connection to your business, then they will not buy your business.

It's just like selling a house or a car. Of course, selling a business is much more in depth, with a lot more moving parts; however, there is still a huge emotional connection that needs to be there. You don't buy a house unless you become emotionally involved in the house and envision where your furniture will be placed, how your yard will look, what school district your kids will be in now that you have relocated, and what this move means to your family. You do not buy the house unless you feel the house will improve your quality of life. You do not buy a car unless you sit be-

hind the wheel and take it for a spin. You imagine yourself driving your new car, picking up your friends or colleagues, and you imagine impressing them. Again, you do not buy the car unless you feel it will improve your quality of life in some way or fashion.

The same holds true for purchasing a business. The buyer must feel an emotional connection to your business. They must see themselves behind the desk calling the shots and making the everyday decisions.

They must feel as if the business is going to improve their quality of life in some way. It may be that they have never owned a business before and they have the desire to be their own boss. The business might give them more time and freedom to spend more quality time with their friends and family. The business might afford them a better lifestyle so they can afford the nicer things in life. The additional income from the business might allow them to send their kids to college. It might allow them to provide a better quality of life for their family. Whatever the reason, it is imperative that you know why they want to own a business and what their hot buttons are. You need to connect their "WHY" to your business and demonstrate that your business will absolutely help them achieve their "WHY" and then some. However, keep in mind that you cannot accomplish this goal if you don't know their "WHY" and if your business does not line up with their "WHY." Below are some tips to engage the buyer and emotionally connect them to your business.

- Ask the buyer to email their questions ahead of time. This way you can be prepared to answer their questions without stumbling over your answers.

- Make sure that all decision-makers come to tour the business. You really don't want to have to show the business again because someone could not attend the meeting. If all parties cannot come, then reschedule.

- When to show the business: Make sure that you show the business when there are no employees or customers in the business. It is hard to concentrate on the buyer's "WHY" if you are distracted by customers and employees. In addition, you do not want to raise red flags by having the buyer tour the business during business hours. People are nosy beings in general. Your employees and customers will ask questions that you may not be prepared to answer. If you have retail or food-related business; then explain to the buyer that they are more than welcome to come in during business hours and act as a customer so they can see the traffic and get a good feel of the business and operations.

- Make sure you have done everything in Chapter Nine in regards to cleaning your business and removing clutter. You should not show your business if it is not squeaky clean or is in need of repairs. Clean your business and make all repairs before showing your business. You get one chance to make a great first impression with your business. Buyers do not give a second chance for you to get your act together.

- Touring the facility. I prefer that you walk the buyer around and show them the entire facility before you sit down and answer questions.

- Discuss different elements of your business when walking from room to room. If you have the buyer's questions ahead of time, then try to answer the questions in the different rooms as it makes sense. If the buyer wants to know the flow of the chiropractor's office, then as you are walking the buyer through the clinic explain the flow as you go. If the buyer is asking if your equipment is in good condition and they are concerned with the age of your equipment, then make sure to showcase your equipment in the best possible light and tell them the age and condition of the machinery as you are walking past the equipment.

- Make sure that if your business has brochures and marketing material to have it lying out so you can give the buyer a brochure or any other marketing material available. Buyers like to touch and feel things. Give them whatever you can as long as it is not proprietary.

- If you own a business that sells food, beverages, or any other type of product, then offer the buyer a taste or a sample of what you sell. That way the buyer can get a firsthand hand glance/taste of what products you sell. They can determine for themselves if they like your products. They can determine if they would do anything different regarding the products. I sold a coffee distribution company several years ago. The seller had a beautiful facility and had a small but very well decorated kitchen. The seller would sit the buyer down at the well decorated table that had an umbrella over it. She would ask the buyer which type of coffee they would prefer to taste. She would offer them café au lait, cappuccino, or an espresso. She would make it for them right there and demonstrate how the machines she sells actually work. She would ask them what type of cream they preferred. Then she would hand them this great coffee that had a wonderful aroma in a beautiful coffee cup on a beautiful coffee plate. The buyers felt like royalty and they loved the products and service she provided. They could see themselves entertaining clients in the same manner she demonstrated. It was very impressive and left a great taste in the buyers' mouths, literally. Buyers requested to buy her products right then and there. Don't be afraid to give away or sell some of your signature products to your buyers. Even if buyers don't buy your business, they could become your next customer.

- Do not discuss proprietary information: Buyers are like kids in a candy store. They want to know and taste everything. They will ask for customers' names, vendors' names, and they will ask for other proprietary information. Simply and nicely tell the buyer that you will be happy to divulge that information once you have an offer with escrow or upon the closing on the business.

- When touring the business, you should stay focused on answering the buyer's questions, addressing their hot buttons, and connecting your business to their "WHY." Many buyers will use the tour as an actual training session on your business. Do not allow the buyers to lead you into training versus touring. Buyers are notorious for turning a tour into a training session. Training takes place after the close, not during the tour.

- Ask the buyer for input on what they would do differently or how they would improve the business: If a buyer starts providing you with feedback on how they would run your business and what changes they may make to improve your business, then this is a very good buying sign! Take this buying sign and run with it, and continue to connect your business to their "WHY!" If not, then you need to ask the buyer for their opinion on how they would do things differently, what new things they would implement to improve efficiency, productivity, and reduce cost. Get them emotionally involved in running the business; get them to connect to their "WHY."

- Allow the buyer to sit behind your desk. Let the buyer sit behind your desk as long as it is clean and does not have any proprietary information lying around. Allow the buyer to feel what it would be like to sit in your chair and make the day-to-day decisions. If the company vehicles are included in the sale of the business, then allow the buyer to get in one of the vehicles, start it, and take it for a test drive. However, make sure the vehicle is clean first and runs well. This process is very effective if you have a luxury vehicle. It does not have the same impact if you have a van or a truck.

- Ask the buyer if they can see themselves running your business. If they can, then that is a very good sign; if not, then you will have to search for another buyer. If a buyer cannot see themselves running the business and performing the tasks that you perform daily, monthly, and yearly, then they are not the right buyer for your business. It is always better to know early on than to waste a lot of your valuable time. When I sell businesses to my buyers, my buyers know upfront after reviewing the offering memorandum if they see themselves in the business performing the task before they even meet with the owner. That way, we are not wasting anyone's time.

- Ask the buyer what they think would be the biggest challenges and obstacles they would have to overcome in taking over your business. They may have to learn a special skill, they may have to acquire certain licenses, they may have never managed employees before. Find out what they feel to be their biggest challenges and see if you could implement a solution to help put their mind at ease. You have to uncover the buyer's fears and challenges in order to implement a solution that will give the buyer peace of mind. If you can solve the buyer's perceived problems and assuage their fears, then the buyer will buy your business. Nip theses fears, concerns, and challenges in the bud early on so you can move on.

- After you have completed the tour and answered all the buyer's questions, do not be afraid to ask the buyer what their next step is in the process. You need to move the buyer along in the process. Time kills deals. Get the buyer to commit to the next step.

Again, get the buyer involved in your business and connect your business to their "WHY."

CHAPTER FIFTEEN

Negotiate Without a Fight, Make Your Offer Airtight

YOU NEED TO KNOW HOW TO NEGOTIATE AND WRITE UP OFFERS THAT WILL HOLD water. Again, less than 40% of all deals handled between a buyer/seller actually close. You can and will waste a lot of time if you do not follow all the steps in this book and write airtight offers. I have listed the steps and considerations that must be addressed in an offer in order for you to actually close on the sale of your business. Miss one step and your deal will fall apart.

Do Not Take LOI (letter of intent)

An LOI is not worth the paper it is written on. It is a complete waste of time. If a buyer wants to present an LOI then they are probably getting that advice from their attorney. LOI means Letter of Intent. Purchase Offer Contract means it is a binding contract. Do you want to spin your wheels, jump through a bunch of hoops, and conduct due diligence for an intent? Letter of Intent means the buyer can back out at any time. Or do you want to go through the process with an actual binding agreement? The answer should be as clear as night and day. LOIs are a complete waste of time,

money, energy, and effort. Have your buyer sign a Purchase Offer Contract. My firm does not take LOIs, unless we are selling larger companies and working with Private Equity Groups. We are not going to have our sellers jump through a lot of hoops and walk through fire for a non-binding LOI.

Obtain escrow money upfront

Most sellers make this huge mistake. They will write up an offer, but they do not collect escrow. How crazy is that? Without escrow money, you do not have a binding agreement. You should obtain a check for ten percent of the sales price. This escrow will be returned to the buyer if their contingencies are not met. You cannot hold a buyer's escrow if you cannot address and remove their contingencies during the due diligence period.

It is very difficult for a seller to negotiate the sale of their business

Let's face it; there are a lot of emotions involved in selling a business. Most sellers have seller's remorse, most buyers have buyer's remorse, and both parties are making decisions based upon emotions, not logic. Buyers will fight to the bitter end to get the best price possible for the business. Sellers are typically not good negotiators when it comes to selling their business. Some sellers will not give at all on terms and price; others will give away the farm. Neither one of these forms of negotiations are good. If you are not willing to compromise in some regards, then you will not sell your business. If you give away the farm, then you have not done yourself or your family justice. There are many different items that can be negotiated other than price. You can negotiate terms, interest, training, inventory, AR, working capital, and a myriad of other points. Do not get stuck on one point of contention. Again, you need to know your buyer and what their hot buttons are and negotiate from a point of strength, not weakness. On average I can obtain a twenty to forty percent higher selling price than the business apprises for or my sellers could obtain on their own. I can do that because I know the players involved, their hot buttons, their strengths, and weaknesses. Negotiations do not always come down to the price of the business; there are many other things buyers consider. Keep in mind that negotiation is an art, and it does require skill and experience.

Negotiate and write up an offer

- **Asset or Stock Sale:** We discussed this in the previous chapter. However, you cannot write up an offer unless you know if the sale of the business will be an asset or stock sale.

- **All Cash or Seller Financing:** Is the buyer paying all cash, bank financing, or some seller financing? If there is bank financing, then the bank in some cases will have the seller's FF&E evaluated as collateral for the loan. The bank will in some cases have their own closing attorney and documents. If you are providing some seller financing, then you must have all the appropriate language in the purchase offer that specifies how seller financing will be secured and how you will get paid at the end of the day. Be sure to check with an experienced business broker or an attorney to familiarize yourself with the law in your state regarding seller financing.

- **Price and Terms:** What is the price the buyer wants to offer? What are the terms of seller financing? How many years are you going to finance and at what interest rate? Are you going to amortize the payments over a longer period of time and balloon the note after five or ten years? What are the payments?

- **Dollar Amount of Inventory Included:** You need to list the dollar amount of inventory that will be included in the business. You need terminology in the PO that states how the inventory will be adjusted upward or downward at closing. You need to have a cap on the inventory so the buyer can afford to pay the difference. If the buyer cannot afford to pay for the excess in inventory then you can seller finance the inventory. Identify how inventory will be taken, by whom, and who pays for what.

- **FF&E List:** The FF&E list should be attached to the purchase offer contract, which will become part of the closing documents.

- **Dollar Amount AR Included:** You need to stipulate how much AR will be included and who is responsible for collecting the AR.

- **Who Pays the Accounts Payable:** This needs to be stipulated as well.

- **Is Working Capital Included:** If you are including working capital, then you should have a specific dollar amount written in the contract.

- **Language Regarding the Lease:** This is typically a contingency written in the PO contract. You need to write the contingency based on whether the lease will be a new lease negotiated by the buyer and landlord or will be a transfer or a sublease. If it is a transfer or a sublease, then you need to specify the amount of rent and terms in the PO contract.

- **Training Included:** You need to specify who is going to do the training and for how long at no pay.

- **Employment Contract:** If you agree to stay on for the new owner, then you need to identify the terms of your employment contract that will be included in the closing documents.

- **Non-compete:** Again, agreeing to a non-compete is very important and gives the buyer peace of mind. You need to specify the terms and length of the non-compete. If you agree to stay on for the new owner with an employment contract for two years, then the non-compete does not go in effect until your last day with the company. Make sure that you check with an experienced business broker or an attorney to obtain specific language on the law in your state regarding non-competes. Every state has different laws, rules, and regulations relating to non-competes. If you do not write the noncompete language correctly, then it may not be enforceable in your state.

- **Prorations to be Paid at Closing:** You need to specify what prorations will be paid at closing, such as rent, advertising, insurance if it is a stock sale.

- **Contingencies:** What are the contingencies? If you allow the buyer to do the majority of their due diligence upfront, then there will not be a lot of contingencies. Contingencies need to be written airtight and they need to be specific. Example: If you are making your offer contingent on obtaining a lease, then the contingency needs to read: "This offer is contingent upon the buyer and the landlord negotiating a lease within a ten percent radius lower or higher than seller's current lease. The lease should not be for fewer years than seller's previous five year lease. The buyer has five days from acceptance of this offer to schedule a meeting with the landlord. The buyer has two weeks from the acceptance date of this offer to negotiate a new lease. The seller has the right to be notified of the meeting with the landlord and has the right to attend the meeting. If the buyer and landlord cannot come to terms as stated above, then the buyer must provide written communication from the landlord within five business days of denial." This contingency is written to hold the buyer accountable to a time frame. This contingency is also designed to make and keep the negotiations with the landlord fair and reasonable. It is not fair for the buyer to think they can negotiate a lease significantly under what the seller is paying. Contingencies are written to protect the buyer but must also protect the seller. Contingencies shall not be written to give the buyer an out or a way to just simply change their mind. The buyer must be committed before signing the purchase offer and putting up escrow.

- **Due Diligence:** You must include an expiration date for due diligence. Depending on the size of the transaction and the contingencies, due diligence can be anywhere from two weeks to two months. The contingencies must be removed and addressed during due diligence. After the expiration date of due diligence, the deposit becomes non-refundable.

- **Determining Allocation of Purchase Price:** This is more important in larger price businesses. However, it is imperative that the seller allocate the purchase price in order to reduce their tax liability. The buyer's advisors will advise them on choosing the allocations for the purchase price. Therefore, this becomes another point of contention in negotiations.

- **Acceptance Date:** If you are writing the offer, you might have the acceptance date correspond with the date that you are actually writing the offer and the buyer is signing it. The buyer might want to have their attorney review the purchase offer before signing it; therefore, you may have to allow the buyer twenty-four to forty-eight hours in order for their attorney to review the offer. If the buyer is going to present you with an offer to sign, then you should have a twenty-four to forty-eight hour time frame in which you have to accept or declined the offer. I provide my sellers with two to three days in which to accept the offer; therefore, they have time to review the offer with or without their attorney and any other decisions makers.

- **Closing Date:** You need to identify the closing date and time in the closing documents. In order to select the closing date, you need to be very familiar with the contingencies and all that is involved. Some closings can take place in less than two weeks, and some can take up to six months depending on financing, franchise approval, and a multitude other factors. You can specify a closing date range of thirty to forty-five days, but it is not preferred. It is always better to have an actual closing date. The closing date can be moved up or pushed back as long as both parties agree in writing by executing an amendment to the purchase offer.

- **Closing Attorney:** You need to identify who the closing attorney will be. As mentioned in previous chapters, it is far better to choose an attorney that will represent the transaction. This method will be far more productive and a lot more cost-effective.

- **Closing Costs:** You need to determine who pays closing costs. Closing costs can be another negotiation element that you should utilize.

Negotiating and writing your purchase offer so it is airtight will eliminate future fights between the buyer/seller and other professionals that will be involved in the closing process.

Please keep in mind this is a difficult task and undertaking to negotiate on your own. It is always prudent to engage a professional, experienced business broker to negotiate on your behalf, which will truly maximize value and save you time, energy, effort, and frustration.

For **ASSISTANCE ON NEGOTIATING AND WRITING PURCHASE OFFERS,** visit
www.betterbusinessbrokers.com
(877) 853-4227

CHAPTER SIXTEEN

Keep Players Focused During Due Diligence

THE SIZE OF YOUR BUSINESS AND THE INDUSTRY YOU ARE IN WILL DICTATE HOW many contingencies are in place.

To obtain an example of a
DUE DILIGENCE CHECKLIST AND CONTINGENCY REMOVAL FORM, visit
www.betterbusinessbrokers.com
(877) 853-4227

There are many players in the due diligence and closing phase. You are the quarterback and it's up to you to make sure that everyone stays focused and on top of their game; if not, your deal will fall apart.

You need to start addressing and removing each contingency so that it does not become a deal breaker. Below I have listed the professionals involved in the due diligence phase. You should start with the contingency and entity which takes the longest amount of time to conclude.

119

Keep Lenders Focused and Moving Forward

If there is any bank or SBA financing in your transaction, then you need to send a copy of the signed purchase offer to the lender. I would not rely upon the buyer to send the PO. The more you control every step in the process, the smoother things will go.

Consult with a CPA if financials and audits are listed as contingencies

Depending upon the buyer's contingencies, you may have to consult with your CPA to provide audited financials.

Facilitate and participate in meetings with the landlord

Nine times out of ten, there will be a lease involved. Do not have the buyer contact your landlord! You need to call your landlord and facilitate a meeting with yourself and the buyer. This is a very important step and needs to be handled as soon as you execute the purchase offer contract. If your landlord will not approve or negotiate a new lease, transfer, or sublease for the buyer, then there is not a whole lot left to do. Before you even start the process of selling your business you should have a good idea if your landlord will sublease, transfer the lease, or negotiate a new lease. Most sellers do not tell their landlord that they are selling their business until they get a purchase offer; however, most sellers have been renting a long time and are familiar with what they think their landlord will do. If the buyer wants to meet without you and you have a solid lease in place, then make the introduction and allow the buyer to negotiate on his/her own terms. Some buyers do not want to negotiate with a landlord in front of the seller. It makes them uncomfortable. My firm participates in all buyer/landlord meetings. We typically will assist the buyer in the lease negotiations. Remember no lease, no closing.

Send PO to Franchisor

If you own a franchise, then you will have to send a copy of your purchase offer contract to the franchisor immediately to start the ball rolling. The franchise approval can take several weeks. Once the buyer is approved by the franchisor, then the buyer has to sign the FDD (franchise disclosure document) by law; the buyer has to wait fourteen days before they can execute the agreement. Upon execution, the franchisor now will set up inspection of the business to make sure everything is up to specs according to the franchisor and the franchise agreement. Most franchisors will have a renovation clause in their FDD that states the business has to go through renovation every so many years. They also have a clause that states the franchise has to purchase new FF&E upon the franchisor's request. Of course, the request has to be reasonable. They cannot constantly add new equipment and expect the franchisee to pay for it. Upon the inspection, the franchisor could tell the seller that they need to update or renovate. This could cost the seller additional money. I tell my sellers if they are a franchise to call their franchise representative immediately before selling the business to ensure they are up to specs on FF&E and renovation. I do not want any surprises for my sellers or buyers after we have an agreed upon purchase offer. If we know the cost upfront, then we can package the additional fees in the sales price of the business or split the cost between the buyer and seller. If you find out about the additional cost after you have an agreed upon purchase offer, then you cannot ask the buyer to pay for it or split it. It is way too late for that. You have to bite the bullet and pay for it. The franchisor will schedule the buyer training anywhere before or after the inspection period. Some franchisors have very long training courses that last for weeks. The buyer should be notified in the offering memorandum before signing the purchase offer of the cost and time frame associated with buying the franchise. Many franchisors also require their franchisee to take a quiz after training. If the franchisee fails the quiz, then they cannot buy the business. In all of my years in business and after selling over 300 franchises, I have only seen this happen twice and it was with a Quiznos and a Subway. In both cases the buyer failed the test on purpose in order to get out of buying the business. Some franchisors will use their own closing attorney; the buyer and seller do not have a choice. UPS is one of those franchises that require buyer and seller to utilize their attorneys. Again, it takes anywhere from 2 to 6 months to close on a franchise business.

Send PO Contract to Attorneys in Preparation for Due Diligence and Closing

Some attorneys are involved in the due diligence phase, especially on larger businesses. You will need to send the closing attorney or attorneys a copy of the PO contract along with the FF&E list so they can prepare the closing documents. Do not have attorneys prepare the closing documents until all contingencies have been removed. If you have the attorney prepare closing documents and the buyer cannot get financing, obtain the lease, or obtain franchisor approval, then there is no reason to have the closing documents prepared. If the attorney prepares closing documents and you do not need closing documents because the deal fell apart in due diligence, then you will still have to pay the closing attorney for preparing the closing forms. Notify the attorney to prepare closing documents after all contingencies have been removed and the due diligence expiration date has passed.

Conduct due diligences

You are in the due diligences phase. Which mean you could be dealing with an audit, lending, landlords, franchisors, or more.

Remove contingencies

It is imperative that once a contingency has been addressed and handled, such as obtaining a lease or conducting an audit, to the buyers satisfaction, then fill out a contingency removal form and have your buyer sign and date the form agreeing to remove a particular and/or all contingencies. If you have ten contingencies, then you must remove all ten of them. You cannot close unless every contingency has been removed.

Review closing documents

Upon due diligence expiration, you will have to review the closing documents and make sure they include the following:

- Price and terms
- Bill of Sale
- Seller's settlement statement
- Buyer's settlement statement
- Lease assignment or new lease
- Inventory amount included
- AR included
- Working capital included
- FF&E list
- Non-Compete Agreement

- Training or employment agreement, if applicable
- Seller financing
- Penalty under default
- Default process
- And MORE

I have seen many closing documents that had major errors in them. These days, everyone loves to cut and paste, so I have seen other seller's/buyer's names, other addresses, and other business names in the closing documents. Make sure that everything is correct and that everything is included.

Time Kills Deals when you are in due diligence. You are juggling a lot of balls in the air all at once. Players will tend to slack, not stay on top of things, and drop the ball. You need to keep all players focused and moving forward; otherwise, you will lose time, and time kills deals, and buyers will find a way to back out of buying your business.

CHAPTER SEVENTEEN

To Close or Not To Close

MOST DEALS FALL APART IN THE DUE DILIGENCE PHASE. YOU SHOULD BE PREPARing for the close while in due diligence. The preparation for due diligence and closing go hand in hand. If you skip any steps or let something fall through the cracks, then you could lose momentum and not close. Below are items that will have to be checked off the closing list as you move closer to the closing table.

Do Not Skip a Step

The Broker

The broker is the glue that holds the deal together. If you do not have a broker, then you better be the glue and hold it all together. It is very hard to concentrate on due diligence, the closing phase, and working in your business, and still tending to your family. If you are juggling all these balls in the air, then make sure you have a good checklist.

Closing Documents

All closing documents must be reviewed one week before closing by:

- Seller
- Buyer

- Additional attorneys, if any
- Some franchisors, depending upon the franchisor's closing procedures, policies, and regulations
- Lender, if any

As mentioned in the previous chapter, there are usually mistakes. Let's face it; attorneys are human too and make mistakes. You want to make sure that all parties involved have reviewed and approved the closing documents. You do not want to make changes at the closing table unless absolutely necessary.

Transfer

- **The franchise or license if applicable:** The franchise agreement needs to be signed, and most franchisors will provide a letter stating that they have approved the transaction and agree upon closing.
- **The lease:** Make sure you have a written lease transfer or a new lease from the landlord. You cannot close without it.
- **Real estate if applicable:** If there is a real estate component, there may have been contingencies on obtaining a real estate appraisal. If there is a lender on the real estate, then the lender's attorney will be present at close or want to use their own attorneys. If you are leasing your real estate to the buyer, then make sure the closing attorney or your attorney draws up a lease for you and the buyer. If you are providing seller financing, then make sure that your attorney has tied the lease to the buyer's performance regarding seller financing.
- **Vehicles if applicable:** The attorneys will need to see the title of all vehicles prior to closing.
- **Bank accounts:** Make sure the buyer has opened their bank account.

- **Credit card machines:** As mentioned in the previous chapter, you needed to transfer the credit card machine so that it deposits money into the buyer's account on the day of closing.

- **Utilities:** Make sure all utilities will be in the buyer's name at closing.

- **Phones:** Make sure that all phone lines will be in the buyer's name at closing.

- **Contracts:** Make sure all customer and employment contracts are transferable to the buyer and that everything transfers over without any issues.

- **Vendors:** Pay all vendors out of the proceeds of the business, and assist the buyers with setting up their own accounts with all vendors.

- **Licenses:** There are a lot of states, counties, and parishes that require certain licensing. There is a small parish in Louisiana that insists that all buyers go to a council meeting and speak to the board in regards to obtaining the required license to start or purchase a business. If you are selling a contracting business or any other specialized business that requires a license, then make sure that the buyer has procured the appropriate licenses to run the business. This is especially true if the buyer is obtaining an SBA loan. SBA requires that the buyer has all appropriate licenses before transfer of the loan money and closing.

  – **Liquor:** If you are selling a bar as an asset sale then the buyer must apply for the liquor license and cannot sell liquor without one. In Louisiana, the buyer must have residency for two years in order to obtain a liquor license.

  – **Video Poker:** Again, if you are selling your business as an asset sale then the buyer needs to apply for the video poker license. The buyer may have to run the bar without video poker because it takes four to six months to acquire the video poker license.

- **Any other:** There are many businesses requiring licenses to run the business such as those listed above. In addition, there are day cares, and many others that need licenses. Make sure you have researched all and any licenses that are needed to run your business. My firm assists the buyer with obtaining all their licenses and everything else required on this checklist.

- Need to conduct a walk through so the buyer can inspect all furniture, fixtures, and equipment to make sure everything is there and in working order before you close.

- The buyer and seller need to take inventory the day before closing or the day of closing. The inventory dollar amount needs to be sent to the closing attorney so they can adjust the settlement statement if necessary.

- All prorations need to be agreed upon and sent to the attorney to finalize the settlement statement.

- Some sellers will allow the buyer to have all the money that came in on the day of closing. Some seller will not and the buyer gets all moneys the day after closing. It really depends on the time that you are going to close. If you are going to close early morning and go back to the business with the buyer, then the buyer should have the revenues for that day. If you are closing late in the afternoon, then the seller should have the proceeds for that day.

- Change the locks or get keys made. In some cases, the buyer wants the locks changed. If you are the landlord, then you have the right to keep a key. If you are seller financing, then you have the right to keep a key as well, especially if you own the building. You will need to get additional keys made and change the locks if necessary.

- The day of the closing. Make sure that all closing documents are accurate.

- Make sure that everyone has agreed on the place and time to close so all parties are present.
- Make sure that the settlement statement is correct.
- Make sure that the buyer brings an escrow check made out either to the attorney or you, the seller. My firm has all buyers make the cashier's check out to the attorney's firm; then the attorney will cut the checks.

Congratulations! You just closed on the sale of your business. That is a huge accomplishment. Now it's time to celebrate—Wrong! Now it's time to train. You want to make sure you train the buyer very well to take over your baby. You want to make sure you leave your employees and customers in good hands. If you are seller financing, then you really want to make sure the buyer is well trained. Train, then celebrate and take your much deserved vacation.

The steps in this book certainly make the process sound easier than it is. I have sold hundreds of businesses and franchises. In all my experience of selling businesses, I have never had a closing without problems arising. I could write many books on all the closings that fell apart and I had to put back together again. Sometimes my career really sounds like a Humpty Dumpty tale.

I always ask my agents and office owners the same question: "When does a business broker's job really begin?" Many agents/office owners will reply, "It's when you set up your listing appointment with the seller." Many will say, "It's when you sign the listing agreement." A lot will say, "A brokers job begins when you locate a buyer or when you sign a purchase offer." All of those answers are incorrect. Of course, our job starts with all of those tasks; however, our job really begins when we have a business under contract and the deal starts to unravel. That is when a business broker's job truly begins. Again, business brokers are the glue that holds the deal together.

If you are handling the sale of your business, be prepared for a lot of issues and obstacles along the way. It is impossible for me to include everything that can go wrong and cause your business not to close. The key is to dot the I's and cross the T's every step of the way. You have to have tremendous intuition, which comes from experience to know what is going to happen before it happens. Once the unthinkable problem occurs, it is usually too late to address and resolve the issues. Not everyone can put Humpty Dumpty back together again. However, based upon my experience, it is my specialty.

To obtain a **CLOSING CHECKLIST,** visit
www.betterbusinessbrokers.com
(877) 853-4227

CHAPTER EIGHTEEN

How to Avoid the Pitfalls of Seller's Remorse in Order to Receive Your Windfall

LET'S FACE IT; SELLING YOUR BUSINESS IS ONE OF THE MOST DIFFICULT DECISIONS you will ever make. In most cases, your business is your child. It's emotional when your children leave the family home and go off to college. You feel a huge sense of loss and emptiness. They call it the Empty Nesters Syndrome. When their kids go off to college, parents typically feel this huge void in their life, and they don't know what to do with themselves. Their daily routine and everything they have done up to now to raise and rear their children has diminished Most parents become very depressed, and statistics show that many parents get divorced after the children go off to college.

The same holds true for selling your business. Many sellers vacillate on selling their business. One minute they want to sell and the next minute they don't. Sellers have nurtured their baby for years and in some cases decades. Typically, sellers change their mind about selling because they simply do not know what they will do once they sell their business. They too suffer from the Empty Nesters Syndrome.

Again, selling your business is one of the biggest decisions you will ever make. However, deciding when to sell your business is the most vital part and often overlooked component of the selling process. Get this wrong and it can affect your profit of the sale considerably. And, never forget that "Timing is Everything!" Let me repeat that – "Timing is Everything!" Knowing when to sell your business is one of the most important decisions that can and will affect your windfall. Most business owners do not plan their exit strategy, and they certainly do not know what the best time is to sell their business. You will need to do some major soul searching as well as proper due diligence to determine if and, most important, when you should sell your business.

Ask yourself the following questions to determine if you should sell your business and when should you sell:

- How long have you been in business?
- Do you still love what you do?
- Are you still passionate about your business?
- Do you still have a burning desire to succeed and lead?
- Are you working on your business?
- Are you still creative and able to continue to grow your business to the next level?
- Do you truly feel like you have a business?
- Is your business trending up?
- Are you growing market share?
- Are you making a profit?

If you answered "yes" to the majority of these questions, then this means your business is still in the positive phase. This could be a good time to sell. You're probably asking yourself, "What do you mean? If I still love my business and it is doing well, then why would I sell?" The answer is because this *is* the best time to sell; when your business is doing well, you still love your business, and you don't want to sell. Most buyers want to buy a business that is thriving not dying. The biggest mistake that sellers make is they wait too long before selling their business.

Here are some additional questions you should ponder to determine if your business is in the positive phase or negative phase:

- Do you dread going to work?
- Are you working in your business?
- Do you feel like you don't own a business, but just a job in which to go to work?
- Are you feeling depressed and lack the passion for your business that you once had?
- Are you burned out?
- Do you find yourself snapping and arguing with your employees, partners, and/or customers?
- Are you having a difficult time making decisions?
- Are you running the business or is the business running you?
- Are you losing market share?
- Is your business trending down or has it become stagnant?
- Are you losing money or just breaking even?
- Are you in debt?
- Are you worrying about your business 24/7?

If you answered "yes" to the majority of these questions, then your business is in the negative phase. It would appear that you have lost the desire and passion for your business. Usually, if business owners are in this state, then the business is not doing well. The business is probably trending downward and/or it has become stagnant. You can still sell your business in this phase; however, it will be more difficult to maximize the value on the sale of your business because in all likelihood your business has lost market share.

Here is the most important question you need to ask yourself: What will I do when you sell my business? It is very difficult to plan your exit strategy when you don't have a beginning strategy. Just like the empty nesters, they want to know what they will do in the next phase of their lives. As a business owner, you need to know what you will do next upon selling your business. You need to write a new chapter for yourself, regardless of whether that chapter is entering into your retirement phase or creating your next masterpiece.

In all the years that I have been selling businesses, I realize that the deal does not get done until the seller has come to peace with their decision to sell their business and create their beginning strategy.

Based upon my experience many sellers have an epiphany within three to six months of the listing process. They will typically call me in the middle of the night all excited about the next chapter of their life. I had a seller (husband and wife) that constantly changed their mind about selling. One minute they wanted to sell and the next minute they did not. About six months into the listing process, the seller called me and said, "Michelle, I had an epiphany last night. I have been struggling with selling my business for months now, because I did not know what I was going to do with the rest of my life. I now have clarity and I know exactly what I'm going to do." I was very excited to hear their news and was waiting in anticipation to hear all about their epiphany. The seller said, "We have always been passionate about bed and breakfasts. We are going to use the proceeds from the sale of my business to fulfill our lifelong dream."

It takes some soul searching to determine what you want to do with the rest of your life. It's very difficult to close one chapter if you don't know what the next chapter entails. Most sellers will have an epiphany regarding the next phase of their lives during the listing process. I typically will spend a tremendous amount of time with my sellers assisting them with their exit and beginning strategy. Many business owners have been buried in their business for so long that they buried their future dreams as well. A good business broker will probe a potential seller to uncover and discover new possibilities for the owners.

Again, selling your business is like parting with your children. Most owners feel a tremendous loss if they have not planned their beginning strategy. Don't get buried in your business and bury your remaining dreams and desires.

Here is the most important question you need to ask yourself: What will you do when you sell your business?

The best time to sell is when you don't have to sell. As I mentioned before, most sellers wait too long to sell their business. By the time they decide to sell, it's too late. Their business is trending downward and the owners are burned out, they are out of ideas to grow and/or sustain their business. These businesses become distressed businesses and are typically a fire sale, which means you will lose money on the sale of your business.

In order to prevent losing money on the sale of your business, then answer the following questions and participate in the following exercise.

Make a list of all the things you don't want in your business and/or life anymore, and contrast that list with the things that you do want in your business and/or life. Example as follows:

Things I DON'T WANT in my Business and/or Life	Things I WANT in my Life
Don't want to own my business anymore	I want to own my life
Don't want to work in my business anymore	I want to work on my business or sell
Don't want to worry about my business 24/7	I want to take vacations
Don't want to deal with employees anymore	I want to spend time with my family
Don't want the responsibility anymore	I want to be free of responsibility
Don't want to be in debt anymore	I will be debt free
Don't want to be under stress anymore	I will be stress free

After you have completed your list of what you don't want and what you do want, then tear up the don't want list and only focus on your do want list. You should do some additional soul searching by sitting in a quiet place and/or meditating on the things that you do want in your life. Make sure you try to unlock what you're passionate about in order to write your next chapter. My sellers knew that they always wanted to have a bed and breakfast. B&B's were their passion; however, somewhere along the way of tending to their children and running their business, they forgot what they were passionate about and they had become very unhappy in the process. Now my sellers are running a very successful B&B and they are delighted. They will continue to run their business until they expire because they do not plan to retire. Many entrepreneurs that do what they love in business tend not to retire till they expire.

However, if you are one of the millions of Baby Boomers planning to retire and you are not sure what you are going to do once you are able to sell your business and retire, then you need to do some soul searching as well. You too should make the same list as above and describe what you don't want and what you do want. You should take it one step further and write out your proverbial bucket list as well. Although, you may want to retire from your business, there are more and more Baby Boomers buying businesses than ever before. I have had many Baby Boomers sell their business and purchase another business from me.

The key is to clearly identify what you want and zero in with laser focus on your wants and desires. Life is too short to waste it on doing what you don't want.

In all of my years of experience I have never handled an emotionless transaction. The entire process is emotional. Sellers have seller's remorse and buyers have buyer's remorse. Problems always occur when individuals make decisions based on emotions, not logic. It is imperative to hire an experienced business broker to facilitate the transaction, cross the T's, dot the I's, and make sure there is no surprise. A good business broker will ease fears, calm the emotions, and keep everyone's eye on the prize.

As mentioned above, when you start thinking about selling, then you should have your business evaluated by an experienced business broker immediately. Do not wait till it's too late. The best time to sell your business is when your business is doing well.

To determine **WHAT YOUR BUSINESS IS REALLY WORTH AND WHEN IS THE BEST TIME FOR YOU TO SELL,** visit
www.betterbusinessbrokers.com
(877) 853-4227

CHAPTER NINETEEN

The Top Ten Mistakes Sellers Make When Selling Their Business

SELLERS ARE TYPICALLY EXPERTS AT RUNNING THEIR BUSINESS. MOST BUSINESS owners know every single intricate detail of running the day-to-day operations. However, sellers do not know and fully understand every intricate detail of selling their business. How could they? Selling a business, as discussed all through this book, is a complicated and extremely involved process that requires a tremendous amount of time, energy, effort, experience, and knowledge of the entire business sales process. Below I have listed the top ten mistakes business owners make when selling their business. Hopefully, this list will assist you in avoiding the pitfalls and common and costly mistakes sellers make when selling their business.

Mistake Number One

Sellers tell people they are selling their business. As discussed in Chapter Ten, this can and will be detrimental to your business. Even if you just tell one or two people that you are selling, they tell someone who tells someone who tells

someone. By the time the story gets around from person to person, it now has been twisted into something that can be even more detrimental. I have heard horror stories about how the story of selling has now turned into stories of going out of business, filing bankruptcy, owners getting divorced and worse. If you are going to sell, the number one thing you need to do is maintain confidentiality!

Mistake Number Two

Sellers wait too long to decide to sell their business. So many sellers wait until they are burned out and have no interest in their business anymore. Then the problem becomes that they do not care about growing their business or even maintaining their business, and their business begins to trend downward. If your business is trending downward due to burnout, then it is not a good time to sell your business. I tell my sellers that the best time to sell your business is when you first begin thinking about selling your business; however, you have not made up your mind that you absolutely want to sell. When you are at the beginning stage—the thinking stage—the business is usually still doing well and will be in much better shape to sell. Remember, it could take several months to a year to sell your business; therefore, you do not want to wait until your ready. By then it is too late. I have always preached to my clients that when they start a business is when they should plan their exit strategy. They should set their business up to run without them. They should take into consideration all the tips in this book and set their business up with the mindset that they will sell their business. Too many business owners do not plan their exit strategy until it is way too late. If you are reading this book and do not want to sell right now, that is OK. You will want to sell one day, and in order to maximize value you must implement the tips and strategies outlined in this book now. Therefore, when you are ready to sell, your business will sell for top dollar!

Mistake Number Three

Sellers attempt to sell their business on their own, and they do not hire a professional business broker to perform the following tasks:

- **Valuate and Price the Business:** Pricing the business correctly is one of the most important steps in selling your business. If you price it too low, then you are leaving money on the table. If you price it too high, then no one will buy. If you reduce or increase the price while the business is on the market, then you send out signals that the business is not doing well and the owner does not know what they are doing. As mentioned in the pricing section of this book, there are many steps, resources, and a psychology that goes into pricing a business for sale.

- **Package the Business:** There needs to be an offering memorandum written on your business that explains your industry and includes all the intricate details of your business. You must have a great prospectus written on your business in order to pique buyers' interest and leave them wanting to know more about your business, and your prospectus will help to eliminate tire kickers.

- **Maintain Confidentiality:** As mentioned throughout this book, it is almost impossible to sell your business on your own and maintain confidentiality.

- **Market the Business:** You need to market your business without breaching confidentiality, which again is almost impossible to do. If confidentiality is breached, it could be detrimental to your business.

- **Qualify Buyers:** The buyers have to be qualified; if not, then you run the risk of providing confidential information to someone that was never qualified in the first place. You also run the risk of someone attempting to gather information from you so they can now go out and compete against you. All buyers need to sign the proper forms that will protect the seller.

- **Show the Business and Answer Questions:** Professional business brokers know when to show the business and how to get the buyer to emotionally connect to the business.

- **Negotiate Offers:** This is a huge step in selling the business and most sellers fail miserably in this step. As mentioned in this book, it is very difficult for a seller to negotiate the price and terms for their business. I have negotiated and written up offers that have taken me hours – even days – to write. If the offer is not written correctly, then in all likelihood it will not close, you are leaving money on the table, or even worse, you are not protecting yourself in the offer. This is not something you should do on your own and leave to chance.

- **Hold Escrow:** You need a third-party company such as a business broker firm or an escrow attorney to hold escrow. Without escrow you do not have a committed buyer and a valid purchase offer.

- **Navigate through Due Diligence:** This is where the deal typically falls apart. It is imperative that due diligence be performed very carefully and the seller's proprietary information still be protected during the due diligence. Due diligence should never be conducted without an offer and escrow money.

- **Remove Contingencies:** If you do not remove the contingencies by utilizing a contingency removal form, then the deal can fall apart and the buyer can wiggle out of the purchase offer and demand their escrow funds be returned.

- **Facilitate the Close:** Remember in Chapter Seventeen we discussed all the steps involved in closing on the business. If one step is left out, then the business will not close. Again, this is not something that should be left to chance.

Mistake Number Four

Sellers hire a real estate broker/agent to sell their business and not an actual business broker. This is a huge mistake and can be detrimental to your business. Most real estate agents/brokers are experienced in selling homes or commercial property, not businesses. They don't have experience in valuating businesses. They do not know how to valuate inventory, FF&E, and AR. They do not have access to industry standards and business comps. They do not write prospectuses on businesses. They are not familiar with all the intricate details of selling businesses. They do not understand and are not experienced in negotiating on businesses; nor are they experienced in working with buyers of businesses. Real estate agents/brokers also do not understand confidentiality. Their motto in selling houses and commercial real estate is "The more you tell, the more you sell." I have worked with many real estate agents in co-brokering, and every single time they have let the cat out of the bag and breached confidentiality. Therefore, I do not disclose any proprietary information to real estate agents/brokers anymore. They also do not post the listings to ten to twenty MLS sites for businesses; nor do they implement a strategic marketing plan. They post to one or two sites and run the ad in the paper very sparingly. If you needed heart surgery you would not hire a chiropractor. Therefore, if you want to sell your business, maintain confidentiality, and maximize value, then do not hire a real estate agent to sale your most prized position, your business.

Mistake Number Five

Sellers do not secure a long-term lease. If your business is predicated on location loyalty and not brand loyalty, then you better secure a long-term lease. Sellers make huge mistakes by putting their business on the market when they are on a month-to-month lease. Buyers will go behind your back and negotiate a lease with the landlord to take your spot.

Many buyers think they can start a business on their own for a lot cheaper than buying an existing business. Also, if your business is predicated on location and your landlord will not extend your lease, then you will not have anything to sell. Secure a long-term lease or a short-term lease with options to renew.

Mistake Number Six

Sellers do not price their business correctly. Most sellers overprice their business, and buyers will string the seller along for as long as they can in an attempt to gather information to compete against them or get them to reduce their price. I have also witnessed firsthand sellers give away their business when I could have sold their business for twenty to forty percent more.

Mistake Number Seven

Sellers will give away the farm when selling their business. They give away all kinds of proprietary information without having the buyer sign an NDA and a non-compete agreement, if one is needed.

Mistake Number Eight

Sellers do not qualify buyers. As mentioned in previous chapters, less than forty percent of all deals handled between a buyer and seller actually come to fruition and close. Most deals fall apart because the buyer was never qualified in the first place. Do not waste your time on unqualified buyers!

Mistake Number Nine

Sellers focus on one buyer only. They put all their eggs in one buyer's basket. If that buyer falls apart, and there is a sixty percent chance that it will, then there is no Plan B for another buyer. Sellers have to start the process all over again when one buyer falls through. Sellers should work with multiple buyers for a multitude of reasons. When one buyer falls through, then you should have several other buyers that are interested. It is also imperative to start a feeding frenzy on your business and set up buyer meetings back to back in order for buyers to see each other coming and going. Everyone wants something they can't have, and when buyers see that other buyers are interested, then they will become even more interested and start competing in the bidding process in order to purchase your business. I have set up several buyer meetings back to back to tour a seller's facility. The result that I encounter is that buyers become more interested and they feel the sense of urgency to put their bid in before anyone else. I have written up as many as five offers on one business and presented them all to the seller. When this happens, buyers start bidding against each other and the seller typically ends up accepting an offer that is higher than list price with better terms and conditions.

Mistake Number Ten

Sellers try to sell to their employee or employees. This is a huge mistake for many reasons. You are treading water and walking a very fine line in trying to sell to your employee. Nine times out of ten your employee/employees do not buy your business for a multitude of factors. Most employees cannot afford to buy your business. I have seen sellers disclose all kinds of proprietary information to their employee/employees that their employee/employees were not privy to when working in the business. In most cases the employee/employees did not sign an NDA and the seller never qualified the employee/employees to make sure that they can indeed afford to purchase the business. The employee/employees now have the seller's confidential information, know that the seller is selling, and know the reason the seller wants to sell, the price of the business, the financials, and everything else. If the employee/employees cannot afford to purchase the business or the seller decides to sell to someone else because they can get a better price or the new buyer is a better fit, then the employee/employees becomes disgruntled and tells other employees that the owner is selling. Even worse, the employee/employees disclose the seller's proprietary information to other employees or anyone else that will listen. In all likelihood, you will now lose these employee/employees and if he or she is a good employee or employees then it could be detrimental to the company and to the sale of the business. Do not sell to an employee/employees unless you have engaged the assistance of a professional experienced business broker to handle the transaction. This way the business broker will cross the T's and dot the I's. The business broker will become the bad person in the employees' eyes, not the seller. If it does not work out with the employee purchasing the business from the broker versus the seller, then the employee will not have hurt feelings, and it does not become personal between the business owner and employee/employees. In addition, the business broker will qualify the employee/employees and ensure that they sign all pertinent documents and maintain confidentiality.

There are a lot more mistakes that sellers make when selling their businesses. I could write an entire book titled *The Mistakes that Sellers Make When Selling Their Business*. However, I thought it was imperative to list the top ten.

Remember, selling your business in all likelihood is the biggest decision you will ever make. In most cases, you are selling your most prized possession. Your business is more valuable than your home, cars, toys, and some sellers tell me that their business is more important than anything else in their lives. It is imperative that you hire a professional to handle all the intricate details and moving parts and sell your business for the highest price possible. Also, keep in mind that selling your business is emotional. Most sellers are very emotional about the sale of their business and in most cases suffer from seller's remorse. When people are emotional, they tend to make decisions based on emotions not logic. When selling your business, you need to hire a professional, experienced business broker that is using logic to facilitate the sale of your business and maximize value in the quickest amount of time possible.

For a **FREE CONSULTATION REGARDING "IS MY BUSINESS SELLABLE?"** visit
www.betterbusinessbrokers.com
(877) 853-4227

CHAPTER TWENTY

The Top Twenty Questions to Ask When Choosing a Business Broker

SELLERS MAKE A HUGE MISTAKE BY DECIDING TO SELL THEIR BUSINESS ON THEIR own. They can also make a huge mistake in choosing the wrong business broker to handle the sale of their business.

When you choose to hire a business broker to sell your business, you've made a very good and sound decision. However, as in any industry made up of people, there are good and bad business brokers. You need to make sure you are choosing a great business broker with tremendous experience to handle the sale of your business. Great business brokers can maximize value in the sale of your business. A bad business broker will cause your business to stay on the market too long and will not maximize value and cost you money.

I have listed the top twenty questions that you should ask when interviewing business brokers. In addition, I am providing you with additional things you should ask for and review before you hire a broker.

1.
How many years have you been selling businesses?

It is imperative to hire a business broker or business brokerage firm that has years of experience in selling businesses. Some business brokerage firms will have agents that might not have as many years of experience. However, if that agent works for a business broker that has years of experience in selling businesses, then interview that owner to make sure that the owner will be working with the agent during the entire process of selling your business. If the owner of the firm does not have very much experience in selling businesses, then do not hire that firm. There are some owners that have never sold a business before and have agents with very little experience in selling businesses. In that case, you should keep interviewing firms.

2.
How long have you been with or owned your firm?

You should ask the agent how long they have been with the firm. That will provide you with further insight regarding the agent's experience level.

3.
Do you work from home or have an office?

There is nothing wrong with hiring an agent or broker that works from home. Although, why are they working from home? Is it because they are new in the industry and cannot afford an office? Or have they been in the business for years and are scaling back?

4.
How many brokerage offices do you have or are you affiliated with?

This is a very important question to ask as well. Not all brokers will agree to co-broker on the sale of your business. So if they don't co-broker, are they part of a national business broker's alliance, and therefore, can co-broker within their own organization?

5.
How many businesses have you sold?

The more businesses they have sold, the more experience they will have at putting deals together. Be very careful of hiring a broker that has not sold very many businesses. There is a reason they have not sold many businesses, and you do not want them to practice on selling your business.

6.
How many businesses do you sell a year?

The average business broker will sell eight to ten businesses a year. If they only sell one or two is it because they sell larger businesses or is it because they are not motivated to sell more or not good enough at selling more businesses per year? Which is it? The answer will be important in making your decision.

7.
What industries have you sold businesses in?

If you are selling a multimillion dollar car dealership and the business broker does not have any experience in selling car dealerships, then you could run into problems throughout the process. It is not imperative for the broker to have industry experience; however, it is very helpful in maximizing values and ensuring a smooth transition.

8.
How many listings do you have?

The average business broker will have 15-20 listings at any given time. If they have less than the average, it might be important to know why they have fewer listing than other brokers. Is it because they are not motivated to obtain more listings? Are they new and that is why they don't have more listings? Is it because they are not good at obtaining listings? Or are they good at selling their listings and that is why they have fewer listings? Some sellers are concerned that a broker may have too many listings. That is never an issue as long as the broker has an administrative assistant and a good support staff in place. Therefore, you should ask the broker if they have support.

9.
Do you co-broker?

We mentioned this earlier. If the broker does not agree to co-broker (and many of them don't) then your buying pool will be limited to that brokerage firm only or their affiliated offices. I would suggest that you keep interviewing and hire a business brokerage firm that does co-broker. The broker should have a fiduciary duty to their seller to sell their business in the quickest amount of time as possible for the highest possible price. They should not have a fiduciary duty to their bank account!

10.
Do you have a database of buyers?
If so, how many?

Most business brokerage firms do not utilize a contact management system properly. They attempt to keep a paper trail of signed NDAs and notebooks. They do not have a proper system in which to sort and maintain buyers. You should hire a business brokerage firm that has a database of buyers. Professional, experienced business brokers will run a query of all their buyers in their buyer databases that could be a good fit for your business. If the broker has a buyer database, then they could actually sell your business much quicker than a broker that does not have a database of buyers in a contact management software program. These brokers will have to sort through paper to find a buyer or start from scratch and advertise for buyers.

11.
Do you have testimonials?

Any professional, experienced business broker should have testimonials and references that you should be able to call. My firm has numerous testimonials. However, please keep in mind that all business sales are confidential and a business broker cannot disclose the information on any sold businesses without the seller's permission.

12.
What is your closing ratio?

Many of my competitors close less than 40% of all offers they write. Those are horrible odds and statistics. These odds are no better than trying to sell the business on your own. My firm closes 98% of all offers we write.

13.
How do you evaluate
what my business is worth?

Unfortunately there are a lot of order takers out there versus professional business brokers. A professional, experienced business broker will valuate your business based upon all the things we discussed in Chapter Eight. Professional, experienced business brokers will not take the listing if the seller's expectations are not in line with the broker's valuation. Order takers will ask the seller what they want for the business and the broker will write up the listing with the seller's dream price without running numbers, pulling industry standards, looking at business comps, and properly valuating the business for what it is actually worth. You can have a high price on your business and let it sit on the market for years without selling. Or you can hire a professional, experienced business broker to properly valuate your business, put it on the market for the best and highest possible selling price, and sell it within a reasonable time.

14.
What resources will you utilize
to valuate my business?

This is key, because a business broker, not order taker, will valuate your business for what it is truly worth, not tell you what you want to hear.

Ask them if they will show you industry standards on your particular industry and business comps to support their valuation.

15.
Do you assist with creative financing?

Let's face it; we are living in a whole new era. Due to the recession and financial debacle, banks are not lending unless the perfect storm has occurred. The perfect storm means that the seller has to have perfect books and records, the buyer has to have near perfect credit, twenty five percent down, collateral to secure the loan, and industry experience. Typical financing is not so typical anymore, and deals are not getting done the old-fashioned way. Therefore, you need to hire a business broker that understands this and has experience in creative financing. Otherwise your business is not going to sell. My firm specializes in creative financing and has been offering alternative solutions for years, even before the financial debacle.

16.
What marketing material will you provide to prospective buyers on my business?

This is a key step as well. Most business brokers do not create an offering memorandum on your business. Most of them do not write any paper except for the listing that goes on the internet. Some will write a one page BLI (business listing information) sheet; very few brokers actually put together a full prospectus. It is imperative to utilize a business broker that will write complete prospectuses on your business.

17.
How and to whom will you market my business?

You need to make sure that you choose a business broker that puts together a creative marketing plan. Most brokers will stick the listing up on mutable websites and that is the extent of their marketing. You need to select a broker that has a buyer database, and does strategic marketing, not just internet marketing.

18.
Who determines when and if you will spend money on marketing my business?

Agents have no voice in how the owner of the business broker firm spends their money. Agents do not spend any advertising money on their listings; it is solely up to the firm's owners to determine which listings they spend money on. If you are dealing with the agent and not the owner, then get clarification on how much marketing and what type of marketing they are going to do on your business.

19.
How do you qualify buyers?

I have seen many brokers not qualify buyers. The buyer signs an NDA and the broker gives them information, including financials on your business, without ever qualifying the buyer. In my firm, we have all buyers fill out a buyer package which includes a financial statement. If the buyer is not willing to provide his/her financials and we have no other way to verify their financials, then we do not provide the buyer with any information whatsoever on our seller's business.

20.
Do you have relationships with lenders, attorneys, and tax specialists?

The number one reason that deals fall apart is because of loss of control over other professionals that are involved in the deal or the buyer's/seller's problems are not being solved in order to finalize the sale. The more relationships that the broker has with attorneys, CPAs, and lenders, then the less problems they will have in that particular deal. I have said it many times: attorneys, CPAs and lenders kill deals. It is invaluable for a broker to have attorneys that they use to prepare the closing documents and close on the businesses. It is imperative for the broker to have relationships with CPAs that they can refer to first-time buyers in order to assist the buyer in the buying process. It is also imperative to have relationships with tax specialists to assist with structuring the deal so we can assist the seller in minimizing their tax liability before the business changes hands. If you wait till afterwards to minimize tax liability, then it becomes too late. If the buyer is obtaining their own specialists and the seller has their own specialists, then the deal will become very chaotic because no one is controlling all the players and keeping them focused on one common goal. My firm has relationships with CPAs and we refer our buyers to them in order to assist them and provide a comfort level regarding valuations, setting up their business entity, structuring offers, and assisting with due diligence items. We have law firms that we work with to represent the transaction and prepare closing documents and close on the sale of the business. We also work with all our sellers to minimize their tax liability. The more relationships a business brokerage firm has, the more control they will have over the deal and their success rate will increase tremendously in their ability to sell your business, solve problems, and ensure a smooth transition. Do not choose business brokers that tell you that they prepare the closing documents and handle the close. Business brokers are not attorneys and have absolutely no business in preparing closing documents! This is a sure fire way to give up protection and perhaps get sued by the buyer. My firm does not prepare any closing documents whatsoever. All closings should be handled by an experienced closing attorney only!

As mentioned many times, deciding to sell your business can be the most important financial decision you will ever make. Selling your business is the most important thing you will ever do. You cannot and should not enter into this decision lightly. You cannot leave anything to chance. It is imperative that you hire a professional, experienced business broker to sell your business. You must not attempt to sell your business on your own. The stakes are too high and you could risk everything you have worked for all these years. In most cases, selling your business is selling your life's work. This is your retirement fund, your nest egg; it is the most important thing you will do. If you need brain surgery, you would not perform the surgery on yourself; if you did, you would die. Therefore, why would you attempt to sell your business on your own? It would be a fatal mistake and could cost you dearly.

Hire a professional, experienced business brokerage firm and perform your due diligence before doing so.

To hire the **EXPERTS IN SELLING YOUR BUSINESS,** visit www.betterbusinessbrokers.com (877) 853-4227

SUCCESS STORIES

I would like to start off by saying "thank you" for all of your help and guidance with the sale of my three custom accessory outlets. **I feel without your support and direction, I could never have received the selling price that you brought to the table. Every step in the sales procedure was overseen by you personally,** allowing me to concentrate on running the three businesses, which were still in full operation.

From the very first step in the sale process, evaluating what price we should ask for the sale of the three businesses, you carefully and accurately helped make those decisions not only easy, but more importantly, beneficial to me, the seller. **You understood all of the intricate details of selling a business** and used that knowledge to procure a timely sale of the business, while ensuring the seller receives the highest sale price obtainable, with all points being considered. The entire experience from beginning to sale, not only happened quicker than anticipated, it brought more than expected and caused very little intrusion, with regards to the ongoing operation of the 3 businesses.

I would strongly suggest to every business owner interested in selling their business to acquire your help in that endeavor. I know that you will make that entire experience not only much easier, but much more rewarding at the closings' sale table. **Your help in this field is invaluable.**

— *M.J., Former Car/Truck Accessory Store Owner*

Let me begin by thanking you for successfully selling our Distribution Company. I must admit that when I was approached by your office, I was apprehensive about being listed with a broker. In my experience, brokers seldom offer the focused, personalized service it takes to consummate a deal within the complexities of today's business environment.

After meeting with you the first time, I could see your level of commitment would be different. After months of hard work and dedication on your part, **you brought me not one, but TWO acceptable offers!** Your unbiased advice during the selection process was also commendable. You made sure the buyer and I felt comfortable moving forward without pressure to sign the deal. **The result was total success!**

In short, you made a very delicate and often invasive process, a very tolerable challenge. Your tenacious, organized and professional style is exactly what we needed to sell these product lines at a more than fair profit. I think you have definitely found your calling. **I would highly recommend anyone who is thinking of buying or selling a business to use Capital Business Solutions above all others.** Thanks again for a job well done!

— Robert, Former Distribution Company Owner

We wanted to thank you and your staff at Capital Business Solutions for the professional and speedy service you all had provided in selling our Cafe. We had worked with other business brokers in the past and now see why your organization is highly recommended.

We were impressed with your explanation on how you determined the value of our Cafe and your marketing strategy in listing the Cafe for sale. It was important that we sell the Cafe for its value and not just for the equipment, as so many past business brokers had recommended. Our Cafe had value in not only its equipment, but also in its 10-year reputation in the Metairie community.

We were very impressed to learn within one week of signing the listing agreement, that you had found a buyer. This was not just any buyer that many past business brokers had brought to us with offers that were not worth entertaining, but instead, a buyer who offered the value of the Cafe and they were good people who we were excited to have become tenants of the building.

Our experience with your organization has changed our negative perception about business brokers. **We would be more than happy to recommend**

your services to any of our fellow colleagues and any person who is looking to sell their business for its value.

— *Raul and Mariela, Former Café Owners*

If you are serious about selling a business or buying one, my personal comments may be of interest to you. In spite of two of my greatest obstacles in selling my business, hurricane Katrina and my health, my business was sold in May of 2006. **I received more than I expected, with 93% in cash. Michelle really showed her wisdom in closing deals and creating a win/win scenario! Her tenacity and focus is amazing!**

Here's my interpretation on how this business was sold in spite of a difficult situation: **Michelle is a true professional who controls every detail of the process.** She is present at all prospective buyers/owner meetings. She does a great job of evaluating the price of a business, qualifying buyers and having them sign the confidentiality agreement. You will never meet a non-qualified buyer. Her office staff does a good job administratively, as Michelle is always working with her clients. They do a good job packaging and presenting the business so that it is user-friendly for clients.

Michelle will do whatever it takes to work for you. She has been to my house four times, and even to my hospital bed! **She works when the job demands it without thought to her personal time. You will come first!** During the many times I was in the hospital, she kept me positive. She always kept promoting my business with such a positive attitude.

I have spent over twenty years as a corporate executive, training leaders to be all they can be. **Michelle is the best example of excellence I have seen in action.**

— *Kirt, Former Medical Exam Company Owner*

I am writing this letter on the way home from my son's special needs school with my wife, Carol. The school is 200 miles away from my home. In the past, this trip was difficult to make together, due to the challenges associated with running a business and balancing a family. Usually, only one of us could leave the business and make the 800 mile weekend trip to bring our son home every other weekend. This all changed when you sold our business.

We want to sincerely thank you for bringing in a buyer. This transaction will positively influence both the buyer and us. It is clear that the buyer benefits with a thriving business and we are enjoying the financial security and freedom to have more time. After all, you should work to live not live to work.

In closing, the transition is going very well and you succeeded in finding us someone that blends in well with the business that we worked so hard to create. **You and your staff are a blessing to our family.**

— *Michael and Carol, Former Dental Business Owners*

At the beginning of the year, I was contemplating selling my Hand Therapy Practice with the anticipation of continuing to work part time in the business as a Hand Therapist versus Business Owner. Initially, my business partner and I attempted to sell the business on our own. After several months, we realized this was a task we were not qualified to handle. Therefore, we met with several other broker companies and interviewed several local and out of town brokers. This was a daunting task as we never felt comfortable with any other company or any other person.

In March of 2010, **we met with you and immediately knew you were the person we could work with and would sell our practice. We appreciated your honesty, professionalism, knowledge of the industry and desire to help us be successful.** We felt you were truly focused on our goals at the same time trying to find a buyer that would meet their needs as well as ours. **In a little less than eight weeks, you sold our business at a rate that was even higher than the listed amount.** The process was handled with expertise and ease and covered all the bases such as: valuing the business, completing the listing agreement details, communicating the process, launching to numerous websites, qualifying/finding the right buyer, securing the financial deposits, arranging the attorneys/legal transactions to finally closing the sale. In addition to your efforts going above and beyond what was expected, your staff was also extremely professional, courteous and efficient.

In closing, I wanted to thank you for all your hard work and effort. I know at times I was difficult to deal with due to my "seller's remorse" as you would say; however, your encouragement really helped me adjust to the transition. I also appreciate your efforts to continue checking on me and the buyer even though the business has been sold since May 20, 2010. **I would recommend you and your staff at Capital Business Solutions to anyone in the future.** My only suggestion to them would be — "Make sure you are ready to sell because it will happen with you."

— *Missy, Former Physical Therapy Business Owner*

I am sending this letter to thank you again for the superb job you and your staff did for me in the recent sale of my business.

At the age of 63, I decided to retire after 24 very lucrative years in the publishing industry. During that time, I published a wedding magazine four times a year, in addition to two large bridal shows yearly. **You negotiated a very satisfactory price and kept the sale in the forefront of your attention.** The result of this effort was a multitude of meetings with perspective buyers in a relatively short period of time and a consequential sale in a very reasonable time frame. Your diligence and attentive efforts have resulted in my retirement proceeding as planned. The efforts of you and your staff have made it possible for me to enjoy a very comfortable retirement.

If I had to do it over again, you would be my only choice to handle the promotion, price negotiation and sale of my business. Thanks again for a fantastic job!

— *Bob, A former Publishing Company Owner*

INDEX

ABOUT THE AUTHOR

MS. TUCKER HAS (AND CONTINUES TO HAVE) AN AMAZING enterpreneurial career; to date she has owned and operated eight successful businesses. In addition, Michelle is founding partner of Capital Business Consultants Franchise. Founder/President of Capital Business Solutions, Better Business Brokers, The Business Doctors and Advanced Medial Rehab.

Michelle Seiler-Tucker is the leading authority on buying, selling and improving businesses, as well as increasing a business's revenue streams. Michelle has sold hundreds of franchises and businesses. She has helped buyers from all walks of life buy the American Dream, create financial freedom and be their own boss and obtain a better quality of life.

What makes Michelle a formidable force in her industry is that she closes nearly 98 percent of all offers she writes, and on average obtains a 20 to 40 percent higher selling price for her clients! Her remarkable track record proves her dedication and persistence; Michelle makes sure the job gets done the right way, the profitable way. While Michelle's numbers are impressive, it's her ability to create win-win situations for her buyers and sellers that guarantee her continued success.

Michelle is passionate about sharing her considerable knowledge and experience with others through her mentoring and training programs. This program has helped many individuals become successful business brokers.

Michelle Seiler-Tucker is considered by her peers to be the preeminent specialist in buying and selling businesses. Michelle Seiler-Tucker was chosen as one of the world's leading experts to co-write the forthcoming book titled, *Think and Grow Rich Today: The World's Leading Experts Reveal How They are*

Using the Classic Principles of Napoleon Hill to Think and Grow Rich Today! Her mission is and will continue to be to serve her clients in such a way as to always deliver more than is expected.

Michelle is truly one of a kind!

IF YOU WOULD LIKE TO HAVE MICHELLE ASSIST YOU IN IMPROVING YOUR BUSINESS, planning your exit strategy, maximize your value, and sell your business, then contact Michelle via the following options:

MICHELLE SEILER-TUCKER

www.betterbusinessbrokers.com
www.michelletuckerinternational.com
www.sellyourbusinessformorethanitsworth.com
(877) 853-4227

Better Business Brokers
A DIVISION OF CAPITAL BUSINESS SOLUTIONS